Cliffhanger

Cliffhanger

Confessions of a Shock Jock

Gareth Cliff

Jonathan Ball Publishers

Johannesburg and Cape Town

© Text, Gareth Cliff, 2016
© Published edition, 2016, Jonathan Ball Publishers

Published in South Africa in 2016 by
JONATHAN BALL PUBLISHERS
A division of Media24 (Pty) Ltd
PO Box 33977
Jeppestown
2043

ISBN 978-1-86842-567-9
ebook ISBN 978-1-86842-568-6

*Every effort has been made to trace the copyright holders and to obtain their
permission for the use of copyright material. The publishers apologise for any
errors or omissions and would be grateful to be notified of any corrections that
should be incorporated in future editions of this book.*

Twitter: www.twitter.com/JonathanBallPub
Facebook: www.facebook.com/JonathanBallPublishers
Blog: http://jonathanball.bookslive.co.za/

Front cover photograph of Gareth Cliff by Albert Bredenhann
All other photographs supplied courtesy of the author and used by permission

Cover by publicide
Design and typesetting by Triple M Design, Johannesburg
Printed and bound by CTP Printers, Cape Town
Set in 11/16 pt Sabon MT Pro

Contents

Preface

Over the years it's become a rather hackneyed jibe – people telling me to jump over my surname. In the biggest move of my life, after a decade at 5FM, I did exactly that: on 31 March 2014 I jumped over the proverbial cliff. It was a giant leap into the future – from broadcaster to entrepreneur, from radio to 'unradio'. It was time to get unhinged. On 1 May 2014 CliffCentral.com was launched.

Many people have wondered: what really happened? Was I fired? Was I pushed or did I jump? Was it an April Fools' joke that went too far? It really isn't a mystery but more of a natural evolution. At age 36, I felt that I had accomplished nothing of real significance. I had done well enough, I suppose, but by the age of 33 Jesus Christ had changed the world, Alexander the Great had conquered it, and Augustus Caesar had found Rome brick and left it marble. I felt like there was still a lot for me to do.

My *Idols* journey continued after 5FM, but in January 2016, after an ill-timed tweet, my longtime Twitter sparring partner, Minister of Sport and Recreation Fikile Mbalula, had this to say:

RSA Min of Sport ✔
@MbalulaFikile

M-net should tell him to go jump over his surname

2016/01/18, 9:17 AM

M-Net listened and axed me. When I won the court case and was reinstated, he duly responded:

I had been asked to write a book about my life and it was something I simply could not do – what was there to write about? I had also been invited by Comedy Central to be the subject of a roast, something I also declined because I didn't believe I had yet earned that honour. I'm really just an ordinary guy who happens to have shared the journey of life with you via the medium of radio and TV. This thrusts me into the public eye, for better or for worse, and that has its pros and cons.

Having hosted a live radio show for the best part of 20 years for three hours a day, five days a week and been on the judging panel for 11 seasons of *Idols*, there's very little anyone who follows me doesn't know about me anyway. In writing this book, and for the benefit of my following on Twitter, I thought we might share a few more stories in more than 140 characters and go behind the scenes to reminisce. We'll go from New York to Knysna, meet funny and famous people, fall in and out of love and get to the heart of every controversy. I'm not usually one to share, but you've bought this book, so now I feel it's only fair.

PART I

My Passion: Freedom of Expression

'I may not agree with you, but I will defend to the death your right to make an ass of yourself.'

OSCAR WILDE

Let's Talk

'People don't understand free speech at all.'

Believe it or not, those seven words caused me more trouble than George Carlin's seven dirty words ever could. By the way, do you know what Carlin's seven dirty words are? They're the seven words you're not allowed to say on television and radio. You'll have to look them up, but the one that doesn't belong there is 'tits'. Somehow 'tits' is one of the worst things you can say on television.

It was 4 January 2016. After a short break over Christmas and New Year, on my first day back at work, I became embroiled in an ugly Twitter party that I unwittingly gatecrashed ... because of those seven words. I really should have stayed at home. But we'll get to that ...

My two decades of broadcasting, ranging from campus to talk to music radio and now pioneering unradio, have been underpinned by my unwavering belief in freedom of expression. It is as close to sacred as anything is ever likely to be for me. Everyone is entitled to an opinion, right? Opinions may be about a whole range of things – what we read or watch, hear or taste, feel or think ... or whatever. Sometimes you will hear opinions you don't like. Sometimes those opinions won't be very nice. Occasionally an opinion will be completely wrong, even unacceptable. Sometimes the people expressing those opinions may even be assholes.

Many who came before us paid with their lives so that you and I could talk as we do now, as equals, across continents and time zones. Throughout history people have been forced to fit in with someone else's opinion of how things should work, but thanks to the Enlightenment, the abolition of slavery, the spread of democracy and the deconstruction of discredited ideas such as racism and patriarchy, as well as increased access to education and information, we are now universally able to voice our opinions. So freedom of speech isn't free.

Here in Africa we're still vulnerable – to militant religion, tribalism, racism and corruption – but *free expression* is the foundation of all the other rights, and the beginning of the solution. If you want to liberate people, you must first allow them to communicate freely – with ideas, with each other and with information. We should jealously guard this right to have and express opinions, just in case the politicians decide to chip away at it again – and they will. Authority doesn't like opinion; it likes obedience. If you don't like someone's opinion and your solution is to threaten, intimidate or harass them, then perhaps the problem lies with you.

In April 2015 I was invited to give a TEDx talk, at the London Business School, which I called 'Africa's New Voice'. The theme of the talk was ... you guessed it ... freedom of expression. As a broadcaster in South Africa, I believe that this is a fundamental human right that underpins all other rights. The right to speak your mind freely on important issues in society, the ability to access information and to hold the powers that be to account is vital to the healthy development of society. We have a long history of suppression of freedom of expression – both pre- and post-colonisation – in which people were excluded from meaningful participation in society, and in turn from the opportunity to better their own circumstances. But things are changing ...

Do you remember how the vuvuzela became a symbol of South Africa when we hosted the World Cup in 2010? While it became a sought-after souvenir at the time, it also created a controversy because of the thundering cacophony it generated during matches. What our international visitors may not have known, and what even some South Africans might not know, is that the vuvuzela is actually a traditional instrument – originally a kudu horn – used to summon villagers to community meetings in rural South Africa. It was a means of communicating, and had to be loud enough to reach people in outlying places. Today, the vuvuzela is mostly used for fun at football matches, and cellphones have become the main means of summoning the people. The cellphone has catapulted Africans into the 21st century in a big way, and we're actually ahead of the curve in some ways too.

Thanks to technology, the true democratisation of the media is taking place. The community meeting, once manifested by trumpeting animal horns, now takes place on the internet – a common area, a public space, just like any village marketplace, except that it is the largest and most diverse space that has ever existed. Anybody with something to say can be heard by anyone else with access to the internet, and this is Africa's new voice.

People get their news and entertainment, connect with their friends, access information and, increasingly, do business via their phones. It wasn't always like this. Growing up in South Africa, we used to have only two options: the state broadcaster, which churned out propaganda and controlled what we could hear about, or international news networks such as CNN, the BBC and others, where we found ourselves listening to our stories, told by foreigners. It was pretty bizarre. Looking at the SABC now, it still is.

Today all the storytellers – from a *gogo* in a tiny village to a smart young entrepreneur in the city – can share their stories with each other and the world, at the touch of a button. The rapid acceleration of social media engagement has made every man and woman in Africa a broadcaster. Digital media puts us in a position to use our voices – and nobody can squeeze this genie back into the bottle. The internet and social media have forever changed the way we interact. Now, in an instant, you can tweet eyewitness news, post a video to YouTube, put a picture up on Instagram or send an invitation on Facebook.

Such freedom, however, requires that we take the positive with the negative – and it turns out there are equal amounts of both.

The Trouble with Twitter

The great thing about Twitter in the early days was that if you said something revolting or stupid or incorrect, there was a kind of peer review that kicked in and you'd be put in your place, as I often was. Mostly, the conversations were fun and mostly they were civil, but even if they got aggressive, there was some degree of rapprochement between parties – ideas were exchanged and things were learned.

Of course the abiding principle was that Twitter was not so much a community as a subscription feed. You'd follow a bunch of people whom you found interesting, clever, funny or strange, and you'd *unfollow* them if you found them distasteful, obnoxious or hateful. Nobody had to force anyone else to comply with government-scale regulation or an enforceable, implied morality. Quite clearly, that has changed.

Initially, Twitter was the global marketplace for ideas and humour, if not the actual public square. Politicians, statists and ideologues were dismissive of social media, so Twitter stayed mostly free from their manipulation and demagoguery. The fanatics stayed in their dark corners, using the old ways.

In 2011, while I was still having fun on Twitter, in an attempt to get my radio audience of politically disengaged young people interested in the very boring State of the Nation Address (SONA), I invented a

State of the Nation Drinking Game. Back when Thabo Mbeki was still Prez, we had tried to launch a game where every time he said 'poverty' we'd knock one back, but his speeches were so dry that nobody could stomach more than a few minutes before passing out from boredom. Jacob Zuma represented a more lively opportunity.

Since many had no taste for the political, I thought I'd see if I could bring a whole new audience to the current Head of State's remarks that start the parliamentary year … by playing a drinking game. These were the rules:

1. You will need a litre or two of some kind of liquid. You may use any kind of drink you like – hardcore phuza, water, wine, beer, tea, soft drinks or even coffee. We discourage the use of methylated spirits, diesel and sulfuric acid, for health reasons.
2. You must watch the entire speech – unless you lose consciousness after the first 40–45 minutes – in which case you are exempted.
3. Every time the Prez says 'Absolutely!', clears his throat or pushes his glasses up onto the bridge of his nose (with his middle finger, as was customary), you must drink one shot of your liquid of choice.
4. If the Prez mentions 'Nquza Hill' or starts laughing, you have to double the quantities consumed.
5. Make sure you don't have to drive anywhere after this game. After all, it's Phuza Thursday – and even excess coffee will render you a zombie.

Viva Democracy, Viva! The game was an instant hit and was trending on Twitter, before trending on Twitter became trendy. In fact, President Zuma tipped his hat to us at the very start of his speech (and for the first time in the history of Parliament) when he said that there were those who 'are following on the Twitter', laughed, pushed his glasses up and cleared his throat. #SONA trended globally that night, and undoubtedly more people watched the speech than in previous years. The tone was playful; we paid attention and we had fun. Nobody had any idea that Twitter would soon become the main platform for political engagement in South Africa.

That Friday may have been full of ugly hangovers, but mostly it was the first time anyone under the age of 30 had ever voluntarily watched the SONA. Mr President, I'm still waiting for my Order of Mapungubwe award …

Those were the good old days of Twitter. In the last year or so Twitter has become a battleground, sadly not of ideas and debates, but of howling, shouting-down, name-calling and identity politics. But I don't want to depress you, because there was one brief shining moment when the threat of something really dangerous brought everyone together for freedom of expression.

During the 2015 State of the Nation Address, Parliament (or the Ministry of State Security – we'll never know) decided to jam cellphone signals inside the parliamentary precinct, effectively preventing the press, ordinary members of the public and even political parties from communicating in real time with the outside world. This was the first sign that the increasingly unpopular African National Congress (ANC) felt threatened, and it was a gross and egregious attempt by them to throttle access to information and free speech.

Luckily, the cries of 'Bring back the signal' forced an instruction to open up communications and order was restored. In that moment, the people of South Africa took a stand, and the government was forced to back down. It was a tremendous victory for those of us who refuse to be shut up or shut out, and it was the first inkling that real democracy was becoming increasingly, and undeniably, entrenched. As I have already said, once that genie is out of the bottle, you can't push him back in.

Back in 2008, one of the early social media adopters, Melissa Attree, told me that I should be on Twitter. At that time I didn't see what Twitter might become, and I actually thought it was quite lame, but I liked the idea that you could broadcast your thoughts in 140 characters to all the people who chose to follow you. Eight years later and almost 1.5 million followers down the line, things have changed considerably.

Lately, people like Stephen Fry and God (@TheTweetOfGod), people who were there from the start and were champions of this newfound platform for freedom of speech, have been cutting and running from Twitter. In a post on his blog (15 February 2016, www.stephenfry.com), he wrote: 'The pool ... is frothy with scum, clogged with weeds and littered with broken glass, sharp rocks and slimy rubbish. If you don't watch yourself, with every move you'll end up being gashed, broken, bruised or contused. Even if you negotiate the sharp rocks you'll soon feel that too many people have peed in the pool for you to want to swim there any more. The fun is over.' Enter the Social Justice Warriors.

I have to say I agree, and since January of 2016 I'm no longer using Twitter the way I once did. It's becoming a bit of an echo chamber, where people only listen to the things that support their own point of view, and attack things that don't.

The lunatics are running the asylum and nobody's listening. Everyone is thirsty for attention and the intelligent and humorous are moving on, to other spaces.

Social Justice Warriors

With the rise of social media, I wouldn't be surprised if business was falling off at the Broadcast Complaints Commission of South Africa (BCCSA). In radio and television, the complainant needs to physically lodge a complaint; each complaint is thoroughly investigated and you have the benefit of a fair hearing. These days, trial by Twitter is instant, and there's very little recourse. In the most extreme cases, like mine, you'd have to seek that recourse from the High Court.

Ironically, having had a long history of complaints levelled against me at the BCCSA and on social media, the greatest controversy of my career came from that one tweet: 'People don't understand free speech at all.' It's true. People really don't understand free speech at all.

What is hate speech? What is free speech? One is protected, the other is outlawed. If opening your mouth and saying a few words can either get you protection by law or arrested by the same law, shouldn't we know the difference? Fortunately there are smart lawyers and free expression advocates who can give you detailed breakdowns of which is which, but it's still open to a lot of interpretation.

The self-appointed Social Justice Warriors (SJWs) almost succeeded in having me permanently axed from the biggest television show in South Africa with that ill-timed tweet during a witch-hunt for one Penny Sparrow. I would never claim ignorance when it comes to the sensitivities of our all-too-evident racial divisions, but I will not try to defend my non-racial, liberal, democratic or libertarian ideas in the face of those who didn't like me before they had evidence of my insensitive timing.

Despite the promise of free expression, the internet brought with it something more sinister – a kangaroo court that suddenly sprung up on your phone, desktop or laptop, with the promise that it's only a matter of time before the SJWs come for you. In the last two years, these digital vigilantes have become so emboldened and drunk on their own sense of moral authority that they feel totally justified in telling your boss to fire you, demanding that the thought police arrest you, threatening the university if they don't expel you and, ultimately, kicking your reputation to pieces once they've done some real-world damage.

The Urban Dictionary (www.urbandictionary.com) defines 'Social Justice Warrior' as: 'A pejorative term for an individual who repeatedly and vehemently engages in arguments on social justice on the Internet, often in a shallow or not well-thought-out way, for the purpose of raising their own personal reputation.' I don't pay much attention to the negative Twitter trends because most of the participants are merely retweeting or copying what the more high-profile 'influencers' or paid Twitter trolls are saying. Perhaps it makes them feel better about themselves by putting others down. I'm sure you've encountered people like this online.

Somehow, by catching someone uttering an offensive remark, they mobilise to catch the low-hanging fruit and create a common enemy. The year 2016 delivered some easy targets after #PennySparrow: #ChrisHart, #JustinVanVuuren, #VelaphiKhumalo, #NicoleDeKlerk, #MathewTheunissen, #MabelJansen, #VickiMomberg, #RiversChurch ... even #BlackFace at Stellenbosch University (which turned out, on closer inspection, to be #PurpleFace).

It may feel like a victory to name and shame these people, but the danger is that we might be distracted from the real enemies, who are hiding in the trenches. The mere allegation of racism carries with it the greatest degree of pain, guilt and humiliation, but the bad news is that racism cannot be totally eradicated, especially not in the Twitter court. If we're to deal with racism, we'll have to dig a little deeper – and pay attention for longer.

In his book *Violence*, philosopher Slavoj Žižek is of the opinion that political correctness and identity politics actually ossify hatred, and have the opposite effect to doing good. While it may render your hate disguised or invisible, it does nothing to change attitudes. Social Justice Warriors have no appreciation of irony, and so stereotypes and clichés are literal and painful to them, rather than being useful tools for the deconstruction of existing prejudices.

It's not only the racists, real or perceived, that are targeted. A month before the Twitter mob unleashed their fury on me in what became #IdolsGate, the SJWs were already baiting me. On the fateful Sunday night of 13 December 2015, after President Zuma had fired Finance minister Nhlanhla Nene and rehired Pravin Gordhan as Minister of Finance, the economy was in free fall around us, and I was called a racist for saying:

The reality TV show *Date My Family* on Mzansi Magic was, as usual, the top trending topic on Twitter that night. Black Twitter, as a group of influencers refer to themselves, is always a hive of activity when these local reality shows are aired. Just by using the term 'Black Twitter', which wasn't even the point of the tweet, I found myself labelled a racist and under attack.

My point is, though, that this same group of people are themselves as nasty and vicious as can be about participants in *Date My Family*, and even more rude about other people's weddings – #OurPerfectWedding being the other top Sunday-night Twitter trender. On our screens we see happy couples sharing their love, and on Twitter we see bitter people ripping them apart.

Watching this on Twitter on Sunday nights is like stumbling in on a tea party of old white ladies gossiping – and since when do we take old white ladies gossiping seriously? It's an established fact that even within homogeneous ethnic groups people find reasons to discriminate. It all comes down to the unfortunate reality of our pattern-seeking mammalian brains and their tendency to generalise at every opportunity. Instead of confronting this unfortunate default setting and correcting it, we look for a temporary scapegoat to send off into the wilderness, our own sins piled upon its back.

Next time you want to venture a comment or opinion online, decide whether it's funny, hurtful and, most importantly, what it's really about. If your own estimation of your value is the motivation for these comments, it might be wise to hold back. I'm willing to accept that I'm not perfect. I have loads of flaws and I don't think I'm better than anyone else – well, okay, better than most … well, okay, than *some* – but I'm not going to be labelled by some SJW who's looking for likes.

If you want to argue your point, it must be an argument based on the facts, not on how someone makes you feel. Unless you *feel* like losing.

Trials and Tribulations

With the advent of social media, and with everyone now having a voice, the confusion around freedom of expression and what constitutes free speech and hate speech is something we will be exploring for a long time. Every time there's another media firestorm about something I've supposedly said, my detractors can't wait to dig up every controversy that came before to prove I'm a racist or misogynist, without taking note of the outcomes. One just needs to delve into the rulings of the BCCSA to discover how frequently free speech is mistaken for hate speech.

After I was axed from *Idols*, in the midst of the legal battle, the *Sunday Times* featured an article about me, headlined 'Gareth's Cliffhanger'. Entertainment journalist Gabi Mbele flew in from Cape Town for an exclusive interview on the Friday before the article was to appear. I was cautious about talking to the press because of a history of being misquoted. Gabi was also one of the first presenters on CliffCentral.com and a friend, so I agreed. Although it wasn't a bad article, front and centre, on page three, was a nicely framed box highlighting my past controversies – just in case people had forgotten what a terrible person I must be. The Daily Vox published a similar list and accused the *Sunday Times* of stealing their article ... whatever ... but here is the summary as compiled by the *Sunday Times* (24 January 2016):

A HISTORY OF COURTING CONTROVERSY:

2004: After little more than a year as 5FM breakfast host Cliff faced his first suspension when he interviewed himself as Jesus.

2009: He tweeted: 'Manto is dead. Good. A selfish and wicked bungler of the lowest order. Rotten attitude and rancid livers – all three of them'.

2010: He published a 1 177-word diatribe titled 'Dear Government' on his website, in which he attacked President Jacob Zuma for fathering several children out of wedlock. He also criticised Higher Education Minister Blade Nzimande, and accused others in the government of enriching their 'family members [who become] overnight millionaires'.

'The ANC believes in "collective responsibility" (so that nobody has to get blamed when things get screwed up), so I address this to everyone in the government – the whole lot of you – good, bad and ugly (that's you, Blade).'

2011: After conducting *Idols* auditions in Limpopo, Cliff said 'the

14

people in Polokwane are charming, but not talented'. The ANC Youth League demanded that he be fired by M-Net. He was also reported to broadcasting complaints authority the BCCSA over a radio interview with an Aids activist in which he said that '22-year-old girls do nothing but lie on their backs with their legs open'.

2012: A complaint was lodged against Cliff over comments he made about suicide bombings in Kabul, Afghanistan. 'Westerners should leave these 13th-century barbarians to blow themselves up,' he said. The BCCSA also received a complaint against Cliff after he addressed a woman on air as 'Dear Bitch'.

2014: He sparked fury when, after the murder of Bafana Bafana star Senzo Meyiwa, he tweeted: 'Who's paying for this massive funeral for Senzo Meyiwa?'

2015: He faced outrage on Twitter for comparing Shaka Zulu to Cecil John Rhodes at the height of the #RhodesMustFall campaign.

Take a moment to digest these. But before we do, I must point out that they missed a couple of big ones – Angry Black Poetry and Watermelon-gate.

Let's start with Angry Black Poetry, a feature I used to have on my radio show on 5FM. I invited the esteemed poet Lebo Mashile on to the show to read some 'Angry Black Poetry'. This is an actual genre of poetry that became popular in the 1960s in America. Lebo was incensed that we had a feature called Angry Black Poetry. Despite being a poet, she didn't know any of this. She was furious and unleashed the old tirade of racism and misogyny at me. She dismissed humour as a blanket for my inherent racism and called blacks who think I'm funny 'Uncle Toms' and 'house niggers'. Her own use of the latter term was arguably more offensive than any kind of Angry Black Poetry we were reciting on my show. The black people who publicly supported me during my *Idols* fiasco were also accused of being house niggers. Fragile collectivism can't stomach dissent.

Jesus

2004: After little more than a year as 5FM breakfast host Cliff faced his first suspension when he interviewed himself as Jesus.

If you're reading this, you probably know that I'm not exactly a religious person. My first suspension came soon after my move to afternoon drive on 5FM. Now, normally if you're suspended from work it's because something really bad has happened or the law has been broken. But in my case it was all in the name of Jesus. I had recently returned from a trip to Los Angeles, during which the movie *The Passion of the Christ* had been released. Everyone was talking about it. When I came back, I did a parody interview with myself interviewing Jesus, the character in the movie.

The next day, programme manager Nick Grubb asked for a meeting 15 minutes before my show was due to start and said that I would be suspended as soon as the show ended. I was in total disbelief. Why suspend me *and* still let me go on air? What were they thinking? I was told not to say anything until the end of the show. I obeyed, well, sort of … Near the end of the show, I announced that I had been suspended for the Jesus interview and asked everyone to join hands wherever they might be and pray for me. And so my two-day suspension began.

Immediately after that, I found myself on the front pages of the daily newspapers under the headline 'Passion of the Cliff'. The BCCSA called a hearing, as they always did for the biggies. I told my audience whenever I could that the BCCSA was the devil. I would write songs about how they had tails and smelled of farts and didn't want anyone to hear really great or funny stuff. At every opportunity I would caricature them as an evil panel of hobgoblins, witches, trolls and vampires.

The truth is, I only ever met them personally once, all of them except the chairperson, Professor Kobus van Rooyen. He had been my Criminal Law lecturer at the University of Pretoria and I actually really liked him. There it is, the most sensational thing you'll read in this whole book. In fact, I can probably reveal now, since the BCCSA will never be able to censor me again, that Prof. Van Rooyen and I actually had lunch together a few times. This never happened while he was hearing a matter of mine, of course, but he had some fascinating stories to tell. Prof. Van Rooyen had his house blown up during the apartheid era by people who thought he was too progressive, and he was also the head of the Film and Publications Board at the time, so he watched a lot of porn and read a lot of filthy literature. He would have made a great radio presenter if he weren't so clever and successful. As much as I've given the BCCSA a hard time, I will give credit where credit is due, and say their rulings are sound. They've actually served me invaluably, in my being vindicated against some absurd complaints.

Prof. Van Rooyen and the rest of the BCCSA sat down to listen to this ridiculous interview, with Jesus speaking in a bad Yiddish accent. I asked him questions like 'How will you feed all the people at your movie premiere?' and he replied 'I'll multiply the popcorn ...' Can you imagine how ridiculous it must be to rule on something as silly as that? Well, these complainants took it seriously. It was a parody, for God's sake.

In the judgment, the Board ruled:
(1) that the interview amounted to satire, which mocked the commodification of religion and not religion itself;

(2) that the interview did not purport to be with the real Jesus Christ but with a hypothetical Jesus who had acted in the film; and

(3) that the interview did not amount to hate speech.

They got it. Hallelujah! The tribunal did nevertheless rule that the interview contravened the time of broadcast in that it should have rather been played 'where it would not be exposed to a wide and varied audience', whatever that means. The long and the short of it is, I won.

Minister Manto

2009: He tweeted: 'Manto is dead. Good. A selfish and wicked bungler of the lowest order. Rotten attitude and rancid livers – all three of them …'

This was my first online bumper-bashing, and came about in 2009 in the early days of Twitter, following the death of Manto Tshabalala-Msimang, our incompetent Minister of Health. You may recall that she was famous for prescribing beetroot, garlic and African potato rather than supplying antiretroviral drugs (ARVs) to the millions of South Africans suffering from HIV/Aids. Thabo Mbeki backed her up in this nonsensical delusion and hundreds of thousands of people needlessly expired. When she herself died, I took to Twitter and said:

Gareth Cliff
@GarethCliff

Manto is dead. Good. A selfish and wicked bungler of the lowest order. Rotten attitude and rancid livers - all 3 of them...

2009/12/16, 15:24

Yeah, I actually wrote that. I refuse to use emoticons in this book, but if I did, I'd put that shocked, blushing face here. This tweet did the rounds on Twitter again (six years later) after I was axed by M-Net, and was mostly spread by the same suspiciously well-organised group of people that I'm fairly sure were acting in concert to distract everyone from the increasingly untenable position of the President.

Back in 2009, and with the benefit of hindsight, I accepted that this was not only terrifically insensitive but also very poorly timed. I issued an apology shortly afterwards to the Minister's family – because nobody deserves to have such a nasty thing said about their parent at their moment of greatest grief. Perhaps it was too little too late, and I was widely criticised and reprimanded. I was told that I didn't understand the importance of death in African culture, that I was a racist and that I was disrespectful of the Minister and her position.

I had to learn then (and there are some indications that I didn't learn well enough) that being right is sometimes less important than how you make people feel. I also inadvertently became the most followed person on Twitter – for right or wrong, controversy has stalked me all my life. Looking back on the whole Manto saga, I would have done things very differently. For some people I was a declared enemy from that day forward, and that tweet re-emerges every few months as an ugly reminder of how freedom of speech doesn't mean freedom from responsibility.

Dear Government

2010: He published a 1 177-word diatribe titled 'Dear Government' on his website, in which he attacked President Jacob Zuma for fathering several children out of wedlock. He also criticised Higher Education Minister Blade Nzimande, and accused others in the

government of enriching their 'family members [who become] overnight millionaires'.

'The ANC believes in "collective responsibility" (so that nobody has to get blamed when things get screwed up), so I address this to everyone in the government – the whole lot of you – good, bad and ugly (that's you, Blade).'

My letter to the government in 2010, which appears in my book *Gareth Cliff on Everything*, seems to do the rounds on social media every few months, and every time some people think it's just been written. Most people agreed with it, but it was the same handful of Twitter trolls who misquoted from it to prove that I was a racist during my 'free speech' controversy almost six years later. Sadly, government has got worse since I wrote that particular letter – and considering the things that are regularly said about him, both in and out of Parliament, I'm one of the President's more polite critics.

You might remember that I had a very cordial lunch with Zizi Kodwa, then presidential spokesperson, after the publication of that letter in 2010. I was encouraged that government might do the right thing and could prove to be champions of freedom of expression, and our other rights. It gave me enough reason to vote for the ANC again at the time. Zizi and I even enjoyed a few social outings after that.

Although increasingly disillusioned with government, I held out hope. That was until I saw the way the Minister of Police and the national Commissioner of Police handled the massacre at Marikana, and until I heard Blade Nzimande's 'Students must fall' comment, and, finally, when I found my confidence rent when the President moved to fire the Finance minister and replace him with a Gupta puppet, not to mention 'Nkaaaandla'. The disdain shown by those in power for the people of South Africa in 2015 was too insulting to bear. By 2016 the tone had become more antagonistic. Even Zizi Kodwa destroyed any credibility he had with me when he joined the online cabal calling me a racist, and when he started calling Democratic Alliance (DA) leader Mmusi Maimane a 'garden boy' among other online utterances. Politics really is an opportunist's dirty game.

Politicians will use whatever they can to distract us; they'll get us angry and promise to make the person who upset us stop; and they'll wait until we're sad at a funeral and speak about how they feel our loss. In an election year, they might even pay a few people on social media to manufacture outrage just so we'll be distracted and forget about a president who faces 783 counts of fraud, corruption and racketeering.

Since my letter, the ANC has been turned inside out in its attempts to protect Jacob Zuma and his network of patronage, and they have lost a lot of support because of it. The most recent municipal and local elections showed not only that the ANC had declined dramatically at the polls, but also that many ANC supporters had protested the vote by staying at home on election day.

The choice is this: South Africans can keep letting events (manufactured or real) divide us, or we can start paying attention to the things that will move us forward, together. If we elect division, anger and outrage rather than adult, rational cooperation, we're doomed. Let's see how the coalitions will fare ...

We are emerging from our political and social adolescence, redoubtable and self-assured. There is still much turmoil. We are faced daily by an onslaught of fear, corruption, threat, challenge and vice. If you read everything, you'll also find that behind the misery of the mainstream media there is also hope, cooperation, dialogue, opportunity and a patchwork unity. It is uniquely ours and it is the product of a diseased past and an uncharted future ... But we are all wrapped up in the destiny of our young, tempestuous land.

Okay. Take a deep breath. Back to the controversies.

ANC Youth League

2011: After conducting *Idols* auditions in Limpopo, Cliff said 'the people in Polokwane are charming, but not talented'. The ANC Youth League demanded that he be fired by M-Net.

In case anyone had forgotten, January 2016 wasn't the first time the ANC Youth League called for me to be fired from *Idols*. After a long road trip to Polokwane for *Idols* auditions in 2011, and some very poor results, my exact words in a newspaper interview were: 'The people in Polokwane are charming, but not talented. There is one person from "Poloks" among the finalists, all that driving and stuff – never again,' to which the ANCYL responded in an official press statement (see below).

AFRICAN NATIONAL CONGRESS YOUTH LEAGUE
LIMPOPO PROVINCE
OFFICE OF THE PROVINCIAL SECRETARY

06 JUNE 2011

LIMPOPO HAS TALENT.

The ANCYL is disgusted by foolish utterances made by Gareth Cliff (idols judge) after the Limpopo idols auditions. The future of young aspiring artists lies in the lazy hands of a mad man. We are worried that what started out as a good initiative to expose talented of young people is losing credibility due to the ranting of one discriminating lunatic.

It can never be correct that Limpopo does not have talent. Instead, evidence to the contrary is abundant. The people of Limpopo excel in all fields. We have produced the legendary Noria Mabasa, Colbert Sokwebo, Selaelo Selota, Peter

Teanett, Paul Ndlovu, Judith Sephuma, Mohlagase, Mopedy, cido, etc. South Africa's leading actors are from our province. The world's fastest woman comes Polokwane. The sitting Miss South Africa is from Limpopo. The greatest footballers of this country were groomed in the dusty sports fields of Limpopo. We have produced Award winning disc jockeys.

Mr. cliff's attitude towards our province is worsened by his biasness against young adults over the age of 28. His statement suggests that if the most talented idol is above his preferred age, he would rig the judging process.

Mr. Cliff represents a small group of backward-thinking ultra-right-wingers who still live in the past. What is more disturbing is that the chap is a radio presenter. This provides him with a platform to feed South Africans with his rubbish.

In trying to rescue what is left of the idol's credibility, Gareth must be released from the panel of judges. The organisers of the event must distance themselves from Mr. Cliff's madness. The youth must not be defocused and demoralized by Mr. Cliff and others like him. Let's all do our best to become the best that we can be.

Issued by the ANCYL Limpopo 6th June 2011

You can't make this stuff up. When the Polokwane episode aired a few weeks later, Julius Malema actually called me after the show and agreed. His words were: 'You're right, Chief, there's no talent in Polokwane.'

Fast-forward to January 2016 and I did end up finding an extraordinary talent from Limpopo – my attorney, Eric Mabuza. Eric grew up in a township outside Tzaneen and went to the University of Limpopo – but more about him later.

Sexism

2011: He was also reported to broadcasting complaints authority the BCCSA over a radio interview with an Aids activist in which he said that '22-year-old girls do nothing but lie on their backs with their legs open'.

One morning on my show I interviewed a young lady called Angela Larkin, a 22-year-old Aids activist who was doing an amazing job helping people suffering from Aids in rural South Africa. I remarked (tongue-in-cheek) that in contrast to her, many other 22-year-olds were lying on their backs with their legs open. It was not a choice compliment, but I run an entertainment show, not a politically correct, identity politics, liberal arts blog. Certainly my comment belies some level of underlying chauvinism, and I'm not at all proud of it, but it set the armpit hair of feminists across the land on fire. One of the Raphaelys labelled me a misogynist and called for a boycott, and a DA councillor called Tex Collins lodged a complaint at the BCCSA for hate speech. You see, it's not only the ANC who fight with me.

Anyway, this case too was dismissed. The BCCSA ruled that I had been largely misquoted in the press (not uncommon), and judged my comment in that context to be completely free of hate speech and not sexist. They even published examples of the newspaper reports to demonstrate the inaccurate reporting. 5FM's station manager at the time, Aisha Mohamed, who went on to become the head of SABC3, said in a press statement: 'In light of the fact that what Gareth said was in many cases taken out of context as well as misquoted, we feel that this is indeed a victory for free speech.' I'm sure there are still a few people in sisterhood circles somewhere who ignore the fact that I wasn't found guilty of anything.

The BCCSA findings were thorough, and worth reading in the light of so many arguments about free speech and hate speech in South Africa:

> To interpret the presenter's verbal image of young people engaged in sexual activity (or drinking) as constituting hate speech would be a gross overreaction. Indeed, to do so would trivialise the very notion of hate speech. The dangers of crying wolf at every opportunity should be borne in mind, especially in the context of hate speech, which poses very real dangers against women and other groups in our society. If the hate speech alarm is sounded indiscriminately, it will lose its efficacy and power in cases where hate speech genuinely exists, and where it needs to be dealt with according to the Broadcasting Code, section 16(2)(c) of the Constitution of the Republic and the Promotion of Equality and the Prevention of Unfair Discrimination Act 4 of 2000. In this instance, advocacy of hatred based on gender is not present. The complaint already fails on the gender requirement. In fact, there is also no advocacy, but simply an opinion which is aired.

The report went on to say that, 'If offensive words are restricted without reasonable grounds, as set out in section 36 of the Constitution of the Republic of South Africa, it would quench vibrant debate, which is an essential element of any democracy. It would, in any case, be constitutionally extraordinary if an opinion were to be limited merely because it is offensive.' I couldn't agree more.

It so happens that this is one of the causes particularly close to my heart, so please indulge me on this issue a little longer. We talk about the 16 Days of Activism (for which I have been an ambassador) somewhere near the end of the year, every year – but nothing ever really happens. Male *hetero-patriarchal aggression* continues to be the mode of operation not only for politicians at the top (paying lip service to women in the workplace while displaying the family values of a character from *Game of Thrones*), but also for ordinary people at the bottom – us. In South Africa, Father's Day shuts Black Twitter up like a sulky child; the reality for many black children in South Africa is that their fathers are either absent or not particularly good role models. What I'm saying isn't even controversial: in 2011 the South African Institute of Race Relations found that 9 million children in South Africa don't have fathers present in their lives.

Of course apartheid can be blamed for this situation. Forced relocations, the migrant labour system and many other factors are at the heart of this collapse in male participation in, and contribution to, the lives of their children. But there is an element of choice and responsibility that should override any decision to have children – especially in 2016. A lot of people growing up in South Africa don't even know who their father is. Knowing where you come from helps you figure out where you're going to. Men have to own up to their dereliction of duty, and we all have to take on the responsibility others have discarded. 'Be a man!', as they used to say.

Bitch

2012: The BCCSA also received a complaint against Cliff after he addressed a woman on air as 'Dear Bitch'.

This was yet another complaint that was dismissed, but at the time caused another media storm. The tone had been playful, but the word 'bitch' is very loaded, especially if used by a man. Sometimes, when a girlfriend says something mean or sarcastic, I use the term, but always in a playful sense and never pejoratively, to put her down. It's like her calling me a 'dick'. In this case, that's why the BCCSA dismissed the complaint, but I still feel uneasy using the word in some circumstances.

Whatever the intention, there's always the chance that someone will interpret your use of the word as a sexist insult, and sometimes that fight isn't worth having. During an April 2016 interview on CliffCentral.com, the CEO of Cell C, Jose dos Santos, made mention of women having a 'bitch switch' during the course of a constructive interview about women in business. The inevitable screeching on Twitter reached fever pitch. There were calls for him to step down, and he was accused of objectifying women. There were even demands for extreme measures, like a boycott of Cell C. Just another example of how your words can cause trouble for you, no matter how much you're actually doing for the empowerment of women or the creation of employment in a business.

For better or worse, the word 'bitch' is actually one of the most common swear words in the English language. Can you believe that as a derogatory term for women, 'bitch' has been used as far back as the 14th or 15th century? It's believed that the definition of a female dog for the term *bitch* was derived from the Greek deity Artemis, the goddess of the hunt. The Romans called her Diana. She was often portrayed with a pack of hunting dogs and sometimes transformed into an animal herself. None of this makes it any more acceptable to use the term, but at least we know where it comes from. In modern usage, the term 'bitch' has different meanings depending largely on social context.

I suppose it also depends *who* uses the term. If a rampantly sexist man shouts it at a woman, it's not like a young woman saying 'bitch please' to her friend. It varies from the very offensive to the endearing. The more men like their friends, the more they abuse and insult each other, and I have rude nicknames for just about all my close mates. Those rules change considerably when I'm addressing a woman, so you can imagine how confusing it gets. What it comes down to is intention, rather than the actual words. If your intention is to hurt, denigrate and worse, then you're probably bad. If your intention is to tease, be ironic or to make people laugh, it can't be inferred that you're beating your wife or trampling on women's rights in your spare time.

Watermelon-gate

2013: A complaint was lodged against Cliff over comments he made about suicide bombings in Kabul, Afghanistan. 'Westerners should leave these 13th-century barbarians to blow themselves up,' he said.

This was another example of where what was said and what was heard didn't match. The actual complaint was that I had made derogatory comments about Muslims. After a news bulletin that reported a suicide bombing in Kabul in which eight South Africans had been killed, I commented: 'There is nothing good in Afghanistan, nor is there anyone with common sense. Westerners should leave these 13th-century barbarians to blow themselves up.' That's it. No mention of Muslims. Case dismissed.

This brings us to 'Watermelon-gate', which resulted in my second suspension from 5FM. During the news bulletin, a clip was played of an interview with a Bangladeshi man whose watermelon stand in a township had been destroyed during a xenophobic attack. The poor man was hysterical, and rightly so. The tone was high-pitched and the clip was barely audible. I wasn't quite sure what I had just heard so I replayed it after the news and said, 'This man is hysterical.' I played it again to be sure of what we had heard. I actually wondered why on earth the SABC news department would play such an incoherent audio clip. The complaint that was submitted said: 'Gareth Cliff laughed hysterically at a Muslim man.' Again, the word 'Muslim' was never used and nor did I laugh. After 'racist', 'misogynist' and 'bigot', the next term Social Justice Warriors like to attach to their enemies is 'Islamophobe'.

I was immediately suspended, again without the benefit of a hearing, for 'religious insensitivity'. That's the downside of being a freelancer at the SABC – there are no rules to protect freelancers. This also was the first and only other time I ever engaged an attorney prior to #IdolsGate. My longtime manager, Rina Broomberg, who remains my biggest critic, was upset with me for being so insensitive as to play the clip several times, but she was even more outraged that I was suspended. She thought it warranted legal scrutiny.

Mark Rosin was then a top entertainment lawyer and is now head of eTV. He and his team prepared a watertight case, and all I can remember was the ton of paperwork and files they dragged along to the hearing. In the end, he wasn't even heard. As it happened, the complaint was against the SABC (since I was contracted to them) and it was up to them to represent me at the BCCSA tribunal. Since they were the ones who had suspended me, how on earth were they going to defend me?

Prof. Van Rooyen was again chairing the tribunal, and we were only allowed to look on as Fakir Hoosen, regulation and compliance officer, and Nick Grubb, programme manager, represented the SABC. As procedure required, the 'offending' segment was replayed for the tribunal.

Prof. Van Rooyen found it difficult to stifle a laugh. He said that it sounded like a parody in the style that people have become accustomed to with Gareth Cliff. By the end of the hearing, it was determined that nothing at all offensive could be found in the entire recording and it was duly dismissed.

Rina wanted to at least claim for the days I had been suspended without pay but Mark said that, the way the wheels turn at the SABC, it would prove more costly in time than the amount owed. We received an official apology. I'm sure it's somewhere in the archives. The SABC had egg on its face – that was reward enough for me.

Speaking of the SABC, since I left, Emperor Hlaudi Motsoeneng has been hard at work destroying just about the last bit of integrity left in that institution. His decision not to air footage of any protests against the government on the news or anywhere else has done enormous damage to the public broadcaster. When Pretoria was engulfed in flames and unrest in June 2016, the SABC didn't mention it at all. The price of that kind of political acquiescence is going to drive them into the ground. My timing was great; I got out just in time.

Senzo

2014: He sparked fury when, after the murder of Bafana Bafana star Senzo Meyiwa, he tweeted: 'Who's paying for this massive funeral for Senzo Meyiwa?'

On the subject of death, in 2014 I unwittingly crossed that line again following the death of Senzo Meyiwa. The Orlando Pirates premier player and goalkeeper had captained Bafana in all four of their 2015 Africa Cup of Nations qualification fixtures. While his career was flourishing, his personal life dominated headlines thanks to a high-profile affair with singer Kelly Khumalo.

It was during this time that Senzo Meyiwa died in tragic circumstances at Kelly Khumalo's home in Vosloorus. Crime does not discriminate and we lost a talented star. At the time I posted this tweet:

> **Gareth Cliff** @GarethCliff · Oct 27
> I really hope Senzo Meyiwa wasn't killed for a
> cellphone. What a senseless waste of a
> talented human life...
>
>   339   136

When I turned on the TV on Saturday morning, I saw this extraordinary (because it was not ordinary – forgive me for being literal here) funeral, replete with marching policemen, government ministers making speeches, flags, banners, food, dancing, singing and a stadium. I have no problem with any of this; in fact I would rather see heroic members of society buried in this fashion than politicians, but in living memory it is *only* politicians who have been buried like this. In fact, some of the great stalwarts of the struggle have had much smaller funerals. This was the first time I could recall when a non-politician had been accorded a funeral so large and impressive. Again, I do not take issue with it, as I normally do with every other kind of misappropriation of state funds. I asked this question, though, and opened a Pandora's box of pretty horrific demons:

> **Gareth Cliff** @GarethCliff · Nov 1
> Who's paying for this massive funeral for #SenzoMeyiwa ?
>
>   368   155

I thought it was a good question, especially because politicians love using a funeral as a soapbox from which to manipulate emotional people. Mark Antony did it at Julius Caesar's funeral and it thrust him into the Second Triumvirate. So if the politicians paid for it, that means *we* paid for it. I don't mind if we paid for Senzo's funeral, but I mind that I am the bad guy for asking the question. I mind it a lot.

My mistake was to ask, 'Who's paying for this massive funeral?' without considering the timing (too soon!) or how many people might have misinterpreted it as something mean-spirited. But the question stands, and has still not been satisfactorily answered. Many other people asked the same question, but my tweet was the one that evoked anger rather than a satisfactory answer. Whatever the responses, I'm pretty sure I didn't deserve 'One settler one bullet', 'Fuck you Gerath you racist pink pig' or 'You and Steve Hofmeyr are the same black-hating peas in a pod' (sic). One again, our esteemed Sports and Recreation minister entered the fray. He tweeted: 'leave him (Myekeni) he is "suffering from a Verwoerd hangover."'

Do you have any idea what a Verwoerd hangover is? I don't, and I doubt very much that Fikile Mbalula could tell you. It just sounds like a half-smart thing to say, something you can brandish as a crude weapon to bash someone's credibility. In fact, it wasn't unlike the nasty weapons other people fashioned to mock Fikile himself about his manhood and adult circumcision.

I didn't ask the Senzo question to be controversial, or because I was looking for attention – and I don't care that my Twitter following went up. I was furious – furious that a famous footballer was dead, another innocent man killed for no good reason. Mobs can kill people too. Terry Pratchett said in *Jingo* that 'The intelligence of that creature known as a crowd is the square root of the number of people in it.' It's a very South African thing to throw the Rainbow Nation into the fire whenever we feel bad about something, but it's a childish reaction and we usually regret it when we're sober.

At the time I wrote on my website: 'I was disturbed but not surprised by outright racism and bigotry – there's a lot of anger in this country, and we pretend to get along some of the time until something awful happens or someone decides to take offence to something in the news. We need to go deeper though – to start understanding each other, and the bad news is that it won't be comfortable. Some black people think all whites are right-wing devils that put on a show and occasionally reveal their real, racist feelings – by being patronising or using language that seems imperious.

'This may be true for some white people, but there are a great many of us who actually really aren't racists – who don't use the k-word, who don't criticise the government because they think black people can't do the job, and who aren't proud of their colonial past. White people need to appreciate that what may seem like a question of fact can make a black person read all sorts of indirect racism and cultural prejudice that cannot be dismissed. We need to talk about our feelings, but we can't be emotional in our reactions. Once we start to understand the other person's point of view, there's a way to turn every cause for conflict into a chance for conciliation.'

The Senzo story went far beyond me. Tasteless remarks about Kelly Khumalo and unkind memes about Senzo's dad with arms outstretched polluted social media timelines for several days, but instead of asking tough questions, we look for scapegoats and distractions. Instead of being sad about Senzo, many people preferred to get angry and nasty – and to what avail? To date, we still don't know who killed Senzo Meyiwa, and there's not a politician to be found anywhere near his grave, house or family. They've moved on, and so have the mob.

Who paid for Senzo's funeral? You did – and I did. RIP Senzo.

Rhodes

2015: He faced outrage on Twitter for comparing Shaka Zulu to Cecil John Rhodes at the height of the #RhodesMustFall campaign.

First, a bit of context around this controversy. In the midst of the #RhodesMustFall campaign, I wrote a blog post on my website, as I regularly do:

When he died, Cecil John Rhodes left some of his enormous wealth to found a prestigious scholarship. Part of his sprawling estate was given over to the establishment of the University of Cape Town and another part to the Kirstenbosch Botanical Gardens, a less controversial but more beautiful legacy. Much of this has been discussed and debated in the last two years, so I won't give you much more of a history lesson.

In recent years (in fact it was a question that arose when I visited UCT two years ago to give a lecture), the presence of a statue of Rhodes had become the focus of a vitriolic campaign against what certain people believed was an offensive monument to a wicked Imperialist who exploited Africans. The latter is obviously true, but then so was the story of King Shaka of the Zulu – who actually killed (sometimes by his own hand) so many Africans that he created anew the map of Eastern South Africa – chasing the Xhosa south and the Swazi north, bringing the disparate Zulu clans under his iron rule. This is not controversial, it is history.

I like the fact that King Shaka has an airport named after him. That doesn't mean I have to like King Shaka. Cecil John Rhodes may have been the most successful imperialist agent of Victorian Britain, but his contribution to history (let alone education) is unquestionable.

Take the Rhodes statue down, I don't care. I don't have a dog in that fight. I'm not a fan of Rhodes and I don't doubt his politics were appalling. As a student of history, it offends me more to see any modern human being let their feelings (however genuine and serious) attempt to cleanse bloody, ugly history of its veracity. I felt the same when they pulled down Saddam's statue and when they removed Stalin's body from Red Square. You can't change the present by whitewashing the past – it's like a child putting a small plaster on his amputated arm.

It is a hollow victory to defeat those already dead. Rhodes doesn't care; the French monarchs whose tombs were desecrated by revolutionaries didn't care and the bones of dead people in unmarked graves are no more troubled by the events of the present than the revered bones of saints. Those doing the desecration however, seldom end up making history themselves. The only way to beat a bad person is to leave your own legacy which makes their legacy look bad.

In the wake of the Rhodes Must Fall campaign, Paul Kruger's statue in Pretoria was defaced; a bronze war memorial in the Eastern Cape was ripped apart; a statue of King George V was doused with paint and a memorial in Uitenhage set ablaze. Since then, Rhodes Must Fall has morphed into Fees Must Fall, valuable paintings have been destroyed and even the auditorium at the University of Johannesburg was torched. This is what we have come to – wanton vandalism and destruction. What a war memorial has to do with colonialism or apartheid is not so obvious – other than the fact that the statues are of white people, I suppose. Either way, I get that same sinking feeling I felt when I heard that the Taliban had dynamited the ancient Buddhas of Bamiyan in Afghanistan. We really do lose much more through destruction than we could ever gain.

People are the products of the time in which they live. We can't judge a person who died a hundred years ago by the enlightened thought and sensitivity of the present. I'm sure people in a hundred years' time will laugh at our attempts at ascribing value to things we hold dear today but which will be laughable in an age of bionics, interconnectivity and artificial intelligence.

Washington, Adams, Hamilton and Jefferson kept slaves, and yet gave us the Declaration of Independence and the birth of modern democracy. Should we destroy every monument, memorial and building named after them because they did what all men of their time did? You can't cherry-pick the qualities of a 'good' or 'bad' person in a historical sense by using your own, or even a modern, set of parameters. By those standards, every human prior to at least the 1700s was at best a barbarian, and certainly all the greatest men and women of history are nothing but despots and greedy oppressors.

How are we to claim the Pyramids, the Acropolis, the Roman Forum, the Great Wall of China and Great Zimbabwe as part of our human story if we pretend they weren't built by the sweat of slaves and the grinding oppression of slaveowners? To hide the statues and spare the feelings of a generation three times removed from the event is to do the actual sufferers an injustice. If a statue hurts you that much, you're giving too much power to the statue.

We have an opportunity to build new legacies, create new scholarships, enhance our world and add to a horrible history by making a better future. Where are the new universities Blade Nzimande promised?

I Am ... Therefore I Think

So what can and can't a white man say in South Africa in 2016? Some people will advise you to say as little as possible, like the big corporations who don't want to cause trouble with government or the loudmouths on social media. I say that's nonsense.

If you're not free to say what you think, you're not really free, even if what you say is wrong. If you're one half the product of your genes and one half the product of your environment, then you can very quickly figure out at least half of who you are from a good look at the family tree.

When we talk about ancestry, we're not very interested in uncles, aunts, brothers-in-law or cousins, but only in those human beings who mated and made you. Fifty per cent of your DNA comes from your mother and 50 per cent from your father, and in turn they are half-and-half the product of their parents. That means that each of your grandparents contributed 25 per cent of your genetic material. The further back you go, the less difference each person in the tree makes to who you end up being, but they all count, all the way back to the approximately 500 people whose combined DNA in 1700 led to your unique presence here today. If you go back a thousand years, it took 8 458 862 592 ancestors to make you. (That's impossible, though, because there weren't even that many people alive a thousand years ago, which proves that we're all related and we're all inbred, at least to some degree.)

People often think that the study of genealogy is a self-indulgent exercise where everyone is out to discover grand ancestors and tales of glory and success. It isn't. Real genealogy is a painstaking, never-ending quest to ascertain the history of your relationships with those who came before you – of the peculiar combinations that produced you – and it's an exhausting (and sometimes very fulfilling) journey into the story of humanity, and your personal story, stretching back over centuries. Perhaps my love of history meant that I was forced to investigate my own personal history. In time, it turned out to be another obsession.

It's a great sadness to me that so many people talk about their 'ancestors', watch documentaries about well-known historical figures, or read about the history of their people, but never manage to find out who their great-grandparents actually were.

My earliest South African ancestor, Wessel Schout Praetorius, landed at the Cape of Good Hope in 1658. He was the first of my forebears to settle in South Africa, and that makes me an 11th-generation South African. That's a long and colourful 358-year genetic presence on the southern tip of Africa for me and my people. Consider that the United States was only founded in 1776, just 240 years ago. At the time Wessel came to South Africa, the Parliamentarians were about to cut off the head of Charles I (another ancestor) and Louis XIV was yet to build Versailles. Genealogy makes history personal, and even though most of our ancestors weren't kings or explorers, they made us who we are.

There's an area of study that's getting a lot of attention lately, and it's called epigenetics. If you consider that all your physical characteristics (eye colour, height, hair, athletic ability and general appearance) are determined by the combinations of the base pairs in your DNA, it would make sense that you should also inherit memories, instincts and character traits in the same way. That's what epigenetics is all about. If the epigeneticists are right, your reactions to conflict, wealth, love, power, pain and circumstance could be very heavily influenced by the experiences of those who came before you. This would go some way to explaining the emotional, mental and spiritual inheritance of Holocaust survivors, the descendants of slaves and the children of those populations who have suffered extreme hardship. The grandchildren and great-grandchildren bear the scars of that inheritance long after the people who actually experienced it are dead. There's another reason to find out where you come from; it gives you a sense of historical context.

I often say to people that this is the best time to be alive, and one of the reasons I give for saying that is that every male ancestor of mine, going back as far as I can go, was involved in some kind of open conflict, and was usually conscripted to do so. Luckily, I don't have to put on a uniform and fight for my king, country or religion as they all did: my father fought in the Border War; both my grandfathers fought Hitler in the Second World War, and of my great-grandfathers, three fought in the First World War and one in the Anglo-Boer War. Before that it was the Crimean War, before that for or against Napoleon, and so on, all the way back to the Dark Ages. It's no wonder men have such a problem finding peaceful resolutions to conflict; we have a preponderance of violence in our inheritance.

Socrates said: 'Know thyself.' Those two words seem awfully easy to comprehend, but they represent a near-impossible challenge in that they entreat us to confront the best and worst things about ourselves, to discover what is true and to mine deep down into our most basic integrity. It's the hardest command in philosophy to fulfil. In asking us to do *that*, Socrates may have stumbled upon the meaning of life. You see, your genes are not molecules, they represent an immortal golden thread of life that, uninterrupted over millennia, link you to the first living single-cell life forms. If at any stage in your genetic history, someone had failed to play their part in the chain, you would never have existed. It's extraordinarily profound. All of this makes it so much more than just a hobby to determine where you come from, and *who* you come from, even if you can only go back a few generations.

Let me give you an example: South Africa in 2016 is fraught with new racial tensions and arguments. We can either look at the recent past or we can choose to go further back, but the more we know about where we come from, the better we can figure out where to go to. In order to come to terms with some of my conscious and unconscious thoughts, feelings and ideas about race relations, I did a little research.

It turns out that I had a four-greats grandmother called Lady Anne Gordon, who owned a tobacco plantation in Jamaica and kept 18 slaves. If we're ever going to have a meaningful discussion about white privilege, superiority complexes or an appreciation of historical perspective, it helps me to realise that part of who I am comes from Lady Anne Gordon. Much nearer to me on the historical timeline, my great-grandfather, the historian Gustav Schoeman Preller, was the biographer of Lobengula, Moshoeshoe and Mpande, among others. He also chronicled the lives of the great Voortrekker leaders and informed generations of Afrikaans cultural history with his writing. In understanding the psychology of the modern Afrikaner, particularly in relation to the English and the blacks, his writings are invaluable source material.

Knowing these things, I can contribute more meaningfully about my own position in an argument or discussion, with less fear of contradiction than if I didn't know. In other words, I'm a few steps closer to knowing myself. That should please the standard-bearers of identity politics, right? Like hell ...

The next time you hear a story about some old ancestor and what they did, pay attention; you're actually getting a few clues to how your autobiography might turn out.

PART II

My First Love: Radio

'Rules of radio – tell the truth and never be boring.'
VALERIE GELLER, INTERNATIONAL RADIO CONSULTANT

Love at First Sound

It all began at midnight in March 1996. I went on air for the first time on Tuks FM, the University of Pretoria's campus radio station. It was the worst radio show in the history of broadcasting, but I fell in love … I think my parents were the only people who listened. Thank goodness.

When I think back to how I tried to impress and put on a radio voice, scripted the whole show, tried to be funny and made a complete moron of myself, I get a pain in my neck. I was so nervous that I remember leaving the studio sweating like those fat men you see on the stationary bikes at gym – you know, the ones in the grey tracksuit material that really shows the dark, wet sweat stains? I was a mess. That first show was so disappointing that I didn't get a single email (though email was only just catching on), and even the fax machine was quiet. There was one fax, from a client of the station who wanted to cancel his advertising campaign. His name was Andrew and he had run out of money, but it might still have had something to do with my horrendous show.

I couldn't have had the faintest idea that, several years and tens of thousands of broadcast hours later, I'd be pioneering my own media 'empire' and that my love affair would have grown into a co-dependent, fully realised marriage. Let's not get ahead of ourselves, though; some people think I should still be on at midnight on campus radio.

Do you remember the first time you *listened* to something on radio? It might have been a song, or a joke or the cool voice of a confident disc jockey. I remember listening to radio when my mom would drive us to school in the mornings. I always loved it when things went wrong – when someone misread something or dropped a tape, or when there was an uncomfortable silence when some piece of equipment broke down. I loved that. It made radio real. I would laugh when callers lost their tempers, when cranky old ladies complained about something, or when the presenter tried to sound happy and excited when you could hear they were depressed and wanted to kill themselves. The slick, smart guys never made me want to listen. Reality TV would come from this kind of broadcast; who knew that I was onto something? I should have spoken up at the time.

The guy who hired me for my first radio job was Rian van Heerden. Rian does the morning show on Jacaranda FM and he is one of the most naturally funny, talented and strange people I have ever met. After an audition, Rian set me off on a path that would dominate my destiny.

By the way, if you ever meet Rian, ask him to tell you about a nasty strip club called the Chip 'n Strip, where elderly, overweight strippers knock themselves out on the ceiling fan while the customers eat plates of slap chips. I have no idea if the story is true or not, but he's such a phenomenal storyteller that you'll wish it was. Unfortunately Rian didn't stay at Radio Tuks for long, but we remained good friends and I owe him a great deal for spotting some tiny spark of potential all those years ago.

What came after Rian was what I called the 'Three Horsemen of the Apocalypse', or, if I was feeling generous, 'Larry, Curly and Moe'. These three made up the new management team. I will not name them, for fear of their teeth, claws and hooves smashing me to pieces in retribution, so I'll give you a little description of each. There was a fierce wire-haired monster I dubbed 'Oprah's eating teacher'. (Remember at this time Oprah was the fattest woman on television.) She was humourless and had a fan under her desk that blew up her skirt and no doubt kept her frigid. Then there was a guy who looked like a sheep. We called him

Crotch. He always looked bewildered. I remember that he liked soft, boring rock music – and especially Toad the Wet Sprocket. What a fucking awful band. Crotch would play that stupid 'Walk on the Ocean' song every day. The final member of the triumvirate we named 'Sphincter Girl' for no other reason than that it sounded rude and undermined her. She was meant to stick to running the news and all the boring stuff, but she just couldn't resist poking her snout into our creative trough.

I know management sound fearsome, but at that campus radio station I also struck up friendships that have lasted a lifetime. We were all together again at a wedding recently and I told them that I think they're pretty fantastic people. Unsurprisingly, they agreed. Many a late night was spent debating and discussing everything from whether the corporation is more powerful than the government to whether Pamela Anderson's breasts mirror the interior structure of the earth – core (nipple), mantle (areola), crust (surrounding breast). My friend Charl and I would meet up at 9 am after his show, go for breakfast in Hatfield, read the entire newspaper, discuss the world's problems, eye out the cute waitress who subsequently became a soap star and go back to campus just in time for my show at 3 pm. Not a lecture was attended, not a scrap of studying done. My poor father. So much of his money was wasted in the late 1990s. Little did I know he would have his revenge by making me pay it all back.

Campus radio DJs are meant to push the envelope, and universities are meant to be the seedbeds for revolution and innovation. I always thought it would be fun to mess around on air with stuff people usually only did in private conversation. I also liked interviewing people who never got to be on radio – people with speech impediments or mental illness. They deserved to be represented in the mainstream media too, didn't they? Not everyone, it seems, agreed.

A lot of DJs just played music. For a lot of DJs, that's a good thing. There was this one guy called 'Dead Air Liam'. He'd play songs and forget to do something when the song ended, so there would be a long silence at the end of the track – sometimes up to a minute long – until this turd snapped out of his coma to say something. He also had no rhythm. He used to sit there with his headphones on, listening to a rock song and tapping on the desk to a completely different beat. Maybe he had a hearing or learning problem, I don't know.

There was a crazy girl with Tourette's who would just lose it in meetings and start blinking her eyes like she was possessed by demons, and then pass out. There was one girl who was doing her show during a violent student protest. While a song was playing she came outside to see what was going on. Jokingly, I said, 'The peasants are revolting.' She went on air and said it. Dim girl. By the way, that story reminds me that we've always had protests on our campuses and that the Fees Must Fall movement is just the latest in a long line of demonstrations by the youth of South Africa. I clearly remember signing up to join every single political party on campus – from Sasco to the Vryheidsfront – just so I could get a free T-shirt from each one. They started getting annoyed when they saw me in a different party's shirt every other day.

I realised at school that I liked making people laugh. I could do a whole bunch of pretty good impersonations – movie stars, politicians, cartoon characters and stereotypical racial and cultural accents that were probably very offensive. In fact, at school that was one of the only things I was good at – because I wasn't very athletic or good-looking.

I've never really liked the way I look – and I'm not asking for vapid compliments to raise my self-esteem when I say that. My brother is dark-haired and athletic and he has good features. He looks like he could be a better-looking version of Princes William and Harry combined, with much better hair than either. My sister is a blonde bombshell, with a brain and tongue as sharp as a samurai sword. I look like one of those tall fish-head aliens from *Falling Skies*. I get up in the morning and look in the mirror and I really believe I should look better than I do. It didn't help that I used to dress really badly and had the worst hairstyle in the history of human hair. That's a possible reason I gravitated towards radio – because subconsciously I knew I wouldn't be judged on my appearance. There are still people who come up to me in public and say things about how I have a face for radio. Although it doesn't hurt me any more, I think my personality only really developed because I couldn't rely on being good-looking.

You're Fired

Radio has always been about imagination. I've said it before; it's Disney's last dream. Radio is the place you get to exercise that one special gift we all have, but use less and less in a world where all the imagining is done for us. The best part about radio (or its online equivalent) is that the exercise of imagination goes both ways. I could describe a tree or an ugly old man and you'd have to put the pieces together in your mind and fill in the blanks. That makes each story personal. Not even the biggest-budget movie in history could do that. Radio really is a storytelling wonderland.

Back in the crude days of campus radio, things were getting a little better: my shows had become bearable, and I was growing a small, devoted audience. Possibly they were all high – I don't know. Then, like a dumbass, I made a dangerous mistake. In 1997 they asked me to become DJ manager. Stupidly, I accepted and for a while became *management*. It was treacherous and I'm still embarrassed. You know how everyone tells you that you should be a prefect at school, and then when you become one you realise that you end up being the asshole who busts the cool kids smoking? It never goes well. I should have stuck to doing shows. Luckily I was too irresponsible to last for long in management.

In January 1998, after a lovely holiday in St Francis, I got back to the station and started my show. It wasn't anything more or less controversial than I had done before: I suggested ways of getting PW Botha to the TRC by luring him with Vierkleur flags like the witch lured Hansel and Gretel with cookies and sweets, and I staged a penis-size contest between a black guy and a white guy we found on campus. I thought it was entertaining. The university and management thought it was obscene. Oprah's eating teacher called me into her office and asked me if I'd like to resign or be fired. I told her to fire me, if she had the balls. It turned out she had a pair of great big, wrinkly, hangy, hairy balls.

Suddenly I was paralysed with fear. What would I do all day at university? Did this mean I'd actually have to study boring *Law*? Oh my God, I'd been fired from a job where I never even got paid. I think I was pretty miserable about the whole thing ... even a little scared. I was just starting to do interesting things on radio; I loved it so much, I loved the people I worked with. I was also humiliated. My parents weren't impressed with my marks in my Law subjects. They thought radio was a passing phase and that I'd probably grow up and become a successful lawyer one day. I've never told anyone this, but I cried when I told my mom I'd been fired. I think she realised how much it meant to me. She smoked a lot of cigarettes that day.

The controversy that erupted in the press was something I've had to live with ever since – as was the moniker of 'shock jock'. All the newspapers love sensational stuff and I knew I had to make a meal of being fired. I was defiant. I lambasted the station, the university and management. I played the victim, posing like Jesus on the cross for the *Pretoria News* photographer.

I didn't give up on radio either. I sent out an amateurish demo tape to every programme manager in the country. Only Bob Mabena, who was programme manager for 94.7 at the time, replied. His letter said something about how there were no positions available, but I appreciated Bob's actually replying. The rest never even acknowledged me. It so happened that much later Bob was the general manager at 5FM when I was suspended for Watermelon-gate. He also came to his senses and left management to do what he does best – a fantastic breakfast show.

I went back to Law, with all the enthusiasm of a death-row inmate. I hated Law. It seemed to me that the only time anyone ever called a lawyer was when bad things were happening or were about to happen. Nobody phones a lawyer to tell them good news, or to share a happy story. It's always divorce, death, contractual disputes, crime or nastiness that attracts lawyers like flies. I didn't want to be involved in misery like that. I remember watching the OJ Simpson trial and thinking if that was as exciting as Law could get, I needed to find something else to make me happy. I still wonder what kind of lawyer I might have been. I quit Law with only a few subjects to go and took up International Politics and History instead. My dad won't admit it, but I think he is still deeply disappointed in me for giving up on Law. For about six years after that, he used to hint that I might want to finish my Law degree. Thankfully, my dynamo of a little sister filled that void. She's now an advocate, and well on her way to making a bigger name for herself than I ever would have.

In terms of disappointment, there was still more in store. I had been fired from my first and only job, I had no money and now this ridiculous dream of being a radio star was the only thing stuck in my head. I tried to get a job – as a waiter at the local country club. I arrived, wore that stupid black-trouser, white-shirt get-up that they think looks smart and went to a table to take my first drinks order from a red-faced golfer who had just come off the course. He didn't look like he had got any exercise out of the round and I was sure he had used a golf cart to drag his substantial arse around the nine or eighteen holes. He barked at me about a whisky and soda. I went off and brought him the whisky and soda. He grunted and said he had ordered a whisky and water. I knew he hadn't. I told him that he was wrong and that he had in fact ordered a whisky and soda. He told me that the customer is always right and that I should pay attention and get it right or I'd lose my job. 'Go and get the manager!' he said. I told him he could get the manager himself, and he could tell the manager that I wasn't coming back. I collected my stuff and drove away.

I was a very bad waiter. Another job I couldn't hold down.

Talk Radio

I was 19, with bad skin. Nobody would date me. I was unemployable and couldn't even do something as easy as deliver a drinks order without having an argument. I was studying useless subjects like History and International Relations, I dressed like Chandler Bing from *Friends* and I had no solid direction. Something had to give. There was also someone I needed to meet.

It was John Berks's last show on 702. I sat in the foyer of the old 702 building and listened to the whole show, then asked them to let me into the offices. They weren't sure they should. The security guard had probably been warned about people like me, and I looked like one of those kids who shot up Columbine High School. Berks had some crazy fans – one of them once tried to kill him with a crossbow – so they were probably very suspicious. They let me in, though, and I met John's producer, Eleanor Moore, a lovely and refined woman who looked like she could charm anyone into doing anything. That's probably how she'd managed to get the best out of gnarly old Berksie. She asked me about my radio career and was extraordinarily kind. She told me I could go in and see John.

I was nervous and in awe, but I managed to tell John how many years I had spent listening to him and how I loved his shows. I recall vividly the long drive to school with my mother, little brother and sister, John Berks and Gary Edwards. It really did feel like they were in the car with us. I think my sense of humour was influenced in subtle and unsubtle ways by their to-and-fro discussions about politics, sport, people and the characters they made up on the spot.

Berks's voice was one of the first ones I had studied and learned to impersonate. He was amused when I told him why I had been fired, and he laughed when I did some unexceptional impersonation of him. 'I'm going to call somebody, she might be able to get you into radio … But I warn you, it's a tough business, and you're probably going to have to do something like produce shows for a while. I'd help you, but you know, it's my last day …' He hadn't really promised anything, but you know those moments where you hang all your hopes on the faintest chance, where you wish upon a star and think about how things might just go your way? That's how I felt when I left the radio station that afternoon and drove home.

A week later I got a call from someone called Rina Broomberg.

In anything we do, sometimes it's either luck or destiny that someone spots you and gives you a break. That's really how I got my start in radio.

There are two kinds of power: overt, masculine domination and subtle, feminine dominion. The one is power; the other is more like influence. Rina Broomberg is not to be underestimated. She speaks softly, she asks a lot of questions and she is very wise. The first time I met her I knew only by her reputation that she had brought talk radio to South Africa, with John Berks, Issie Kirsh and Stan Katz. She had been station manager of 702 at its height in the late 1980s and early 1990s and knew what listeners wanted. She also knew how to manage talent, which is said to be akin to herding cats – something nobody has ever actually tried to do, but which is likely impossible. At the time I met her, Rina was consulting to a powerful advertising agency, and wasn't involved in radio at all, but she took the time to listen to my story and hear all the stupid ideas I had for my own show. I had lists and lists of ideas. Some of them were so ridiculous that I'm sure she thought I was nuts. Somehow, as life worked out, a few months later she gave me my break on commercial radio.

Between calls made by John and Rina to 702, they persuaded someone to take me on as an intern. I was earning less money than my petrol cost each month and doing research and a little bit of production for shows that I found really boring. For a while I assisted with production on various shows, including veteran broadcasters such as John Robbie, Jenny Crwys-Williams and Barry Ronge, but I was a useless producer. The only show I enjoyed working on at that time was Kate Turkington's *Believe It Or Not* – a show that ran for 20 years and was always inspiring and/or thought-provoking. The rest of them were so depressing that I almost gave up on radio completely – presenters having manufactured, serious, dry conversations with self-absorbed and annoying listeners. To me, it started to sound like an old-age home on the air. You could almost smell that pee smell you get in retirement village passages.

During this time, however, I did start something I'm still proud of, even though it didn't last long. It was also my first venture into the online world, perhaps a precursor of what was to come all these years later. A friend of mine, and another intern at 702, John Kuhn (who most unfortunately left us suddenly in his prime due to a heart ailment), and I started a student website called gAL.co.za. It was a fun site for entertainment, info, cool games and other student-related material. We managed to gain international notoriety with a game where you could squirt diesel at Robert Mugabe, which coincided with the fuel crisis that country was experiencing. It made the pages of *Time* magazine and got us direct threats from the Zimbabwean government. We had high hopes for the site and we worked hard to keep it fresh and edgy, but the big internet crash that came in 2000 tore up our hopes of selling the business for a massive profit.

A highlight of my 702 intern days was working on the 1999 election. Another intern at 702, Alan Ford, and I were charged with being gofers for the news department as 702 geared up for its renowned extensive coverage of such important events. On the night the results were announced, we congratulated President-elect Thabo Mbeki and danced with Nkosazana Dlamini-Zuma at the hastily arranged afterparty. I may have been the first person to address Thabo as 'Mr President', immediately after the announcement and as he turned to go up the stairs. That's how I remember it, anyway. But the story gets better …

A few nights later, I was at home messing around and got a call from Alan: 'Get dressed, wear a tux, I'm picking you up in 25 minutes.' Alan had clearly come up with some dodgy plan. On the way to Pretoria he told me we were going to sneak into the Presidential Inauguration banquet, on Strydom Square. I told him he was mad. The likes of Prince Charles and Nelson Mandela would be there. 'There's no way you can sneak into an event that big! It'll be crawling with security!' I said. Alan instructed me just to follow his lead. While his tactics may have been questionable, I knew enough to know that Alan was the one person who could hustle his way into anything – but even I had my doubts this time.

We parked some distance away and walked up to the entrance with all the other VIPs. Like a slick professional, Alan sidled up to Mbhazima Shilowa, who was about to become Premier of Gauteng. 'Mbhazeeeema!' he cooed, 'how aaaaaare you, my friend?', and in one swift movement, we sashayed, laughed and chatted our way right past security, in Shilowa's wake. After bullshitting our way to Table 22 with Richard Branson, the Jamaican Ambassador, Aziz Pahad and his wife, and some other vaguely familiar celebrities, we sat there, self-satisfied and not a bit out of place, talking to everyone as if we were absolutely meant to be there.

In this rarified atmosphere of VVVIPs, heads of state, diplomats and supremely powerful businesspeople, sat Gareth 'Nobody' Cliff and Alan 'S'dudla' Ford. Massive chandeliers, lavish table decorations, free drink and food and not a single question all night about who we were or why we were there – it was stupendous! I will always credit Alan with the ability to schmooze his way into absolutely anything, and this was his *coup de grâce*. As a student of history, I shall never forget Nelson Mandela's speech, Thabo Mbeki's first speech as President, and meeting the late Muammar Gadaffi, Yasser Arafat and many other people I was unlikely to encounter just about anywhere or at any time.

Once the experience of the election was over, it was back to being a call-screener for mostly boring calls, and I didn't see that I had any future in radio. In the late 1990s, 702 was going through a tough time: it was still broadcasting on AM (MW) while a lot more SABC radio stations had been privatised. The competition was fierce. Primedia-owned 702 took a direct hit with the purchase of 94.7 Highveld Stereo as sister station, and Jeremy Mansfield moved from 702 to host the breakfast show on Highveld. Luckily they decided to bring Rina back as managing director.

My Big Break

Rina joined in August 1999, the month I turned 22. In order to attract some positive attention for 702 again, she initiated a major shake-up. After interviewing every member of staff, she changed the line-up and started the 'nursery school', as she called it, putting fresh voices on air during the all-night shift. People started talking about 702 again. She also brought John Berks back to the breakfast show, with John Robbie hosting afternoon drive, and she put me on after midnight. She said I had 'potential'. To this day, that's the biggest compliment she's ever given me. At least I always knew she meant it.

I was thrilled to have space to play again. I started my show by having a fight with an old bag called Anne M Stommel. She called me a cheeky young 'whippersnapper' with too many opinions and I snapped back. I really unleashed hell on this poor lady. I told her she was old and irrelevant. We started yelling at each other on air and she told me she was going to write a stern letter to management. Suddenly I was back in business! And Anne became a regular caller.

That adrenaline rush, the feeling you get when you know you're on the edge, on air, is the most exciting feeling in the world. It's not always the controversial, shocking, crazy things that make you feel that way, but you know that anyone who is listening isn't going to switch off when something really exciting happens. After midnight you get all the crazies phoning in, and I was having the time of my life. Business at the Broadcasting Complaints Commission of South Africa (BCCSA) picked up considerably.

After a fairly short stint on the all-night show I was moved to an hour in the afternoon from 3 to 4 pm, after Alec Hogg, who hosted a very successful hour-long business show, left abruptly. I do believe that the insomniac old ladies missed me ... and I missed them. Now I had to be more focused, and I even got my own producer. The BCCSA complaints continued to pour in and Rina continued to support me, using my age and inexperience as a way of explaining away the risqué (and sometimes stupid) stuff I was doing on air.

Most of the complaints had been minor and all were dismissed, but I knew that the first major hearing couldn't be far away. I didn't have to wait long ... My producer, Duduzile Moseneke, mentioned in passing that Shangaan men have bigger penises than any other group in South

Africa – well, that was the urban (or rural) legend. The station manager at the time, Dan Moyane, is Shangaan and I said that we had the best-hung station manager on the planet. Someone complained that I was bringing up unnecessary tribalism and sent us off to the BCCSA.

Poor Dan had to defend me in front of Professor Kobus van Rooyen and the tribunal while I was on my first trip to New York. Fortunately he didn't have to show any personal anatomical evidence and the case was dismissed. I didn't know that at the time, because while Dan was talking about penises I was telling my story to Howard Stern and his 16 million listeners.

I went to New York to attend a broadcasting convention in preparation for taking over the morning show from John Berks. There was someone I was determined to meet. If there was ever anyone in radio I really looked up to, it was Howard Stern. I had seen his movie, *Private Parts*, and I think he opened my ears to the kinds of real, honest things that you hardly ever hear on radio in South Africa. I had never heard his shows but I knew he was an innovator. I took a chance and called up Howard's producer, Gary Dell'Abate. He arranged for me to visit *The Howard Stern Show*. Not at all expecting to be interviewed, as I walked into the studio they started playing African xylophone music and Howard said: 'So this DJ, talk show host from South Africa, Gareth Cliff, has just been carried in by six black slaves …' Right off the bat he asked me why the whites had given up on apartheid, since it was working so well for us. He asked me what apartheid was like. I looked around and told him that it was almost like his studio, with all the white people in the main studio and his co-host Robin (who is black) in her own booth. He laughed, but I knew I was in the lion's den and a mixture of nerves and excitement took over. In the end, Howard was almost fatherly, taking off his glasses and talking to me about radio, like you'd talk to a friend. I'm often asked if there is anyone I would still like to interview. It would probably be Howard Stern.

That trip to New York, my first, was exactly a year before 9/11 – the day the world changed. Being at a talk radio station when major breaking news happens is exhilarating: you're at the nexus of all the incoming and outgoing information, and you're the point of contact for people who are on the scene, reacting and sharing their feelings as things happen. At 702, the whole place sprang into action on 9/11, and nobody was quite sure what was happening until the second plane hit the World Trade Center. Since that day, a question that almost everyone can answer is 'Where were you on 11 September 2001?' I remember how profoundly the events of that day affected me, and how they shook the foundations of civilisation.

When major world events like that happen, you learn a lot, really fast. My baptism by fire was still ahead ...

Out of the Frying Pan

My move across the 702 time slots was rapid. John Berks was doing the breakfast show in 2000 and decided he had had enough of early mornings. Rina admitted later that she took the biggest risk of her professional life by putting me on this prime slot to replace the legendary Berksie, but it was time to attract a new audience. Nevertheless, these were the biggest shoes anyone could fill in the history of South African broadcasting. When I took over from John he said some nice things but reminded me how the audience would probably hate me for at least a few months. And so would some of my fellow more-seasoned broadcasters ...

Rina put the station's advertising budget money where her mouth was and launched a cheeky billboard campaign with my photograph and the slogan, 'The New Face of Radio'. Another billboard that infuriated our sister station, 94.7 Highveld Stereo, had the slogan 'Daily relief from the dry Highveld'. A third billboard read: 'Start your day with a shave, a shower and a little shit.' That one was placed on William Nicol Drive, a major thoroughfare in Bryanston, and caused considerable outrage. The Advertising Standards Authority decided it was unacceptable – the guerrilla marketing ploy had worked. This was used as a major PR opportunity and I had to get up on a big ladder and have pictures taken of me spray-painting over the word 'shit' and replacing it with the word 'shirt'.

From that point on, I went from being the naughty new kid on the block who was friendly with everyone to being a threat to some of the more established names. Many of my colleagues either outright ignored me or were overly sweet, secretly hoping that I would fail. Rina also had a hard time in meetings, but she only told me about that a few years later. I was 23, doing a show with an audience whose average age was that of my parents, and I was attracting attention. SAfm put out an ad with a picture of a nappy and the line: 'We don't need to change our presenters.' Fuck you, I thought, I'm going to make this work. I'm going to win.

My first show started with a prayer for tremendous ratings and for all the other morning shows to get sick with rashes and infestations of pubic lice. I think I was a prize brat, but I didn't know it at the time. That being said, I can still be a prize brat. It was a wild ride, with Rina and the team trying to produce a semblance of consistency while I earned the title of 'shock jock'. It was never one I really identified with. If someone is a shock jock, they're usually doing just about anything to get attention. I have always had a keen interest in real conversation, in argument, in different points of view and in developing and refining my opinions. Being funny and being brutally honest was always part of the formulation of those opinions, but I wasn't looking to be a comedian. There were some things I cared about – South Africa and our place in the world, free speech, irony, humour, leaving something positive where I found something negative. It sounds trite now, but I was a deeply ideological young man.

One morning at six, just after I had described the sun rising over the East Rand, I received a call from a man who sounded a bit emotional and thanked me for describing the sunrise. When I spoke about the view through our east-facing window that morning, I hadn't thought much of it; I just talked about the colours and the chimneys and the birds. I was probably filling up the time because I needed to get to news or traffic on time. I thought it was very strange that this caller had brought it up and so I became dismissive. I was about to cut him off when he stopped me and said, 'No, Gareth, thank you for telling me what it looks like … you see, I'm blind.' I got a lump in my throat. My voice croaked a little as I thanked him and took a break. It's at moments like that when you realise how privileged you are to be allowed into people's lives, and how the slightest word, tone or description can do wonderful or terrible things.

It's amazing what we can see with our ears.

702 Breakfast Show

The morning show was a steep learning curve, and I can admit now that I put on a lot of false bravado when I was actually quite insecure and vulnerable. What the hell does any 23-year-old know about branding, PR, corporate jealousy and boardroom politics, especially when that 23-year-old is given latitude to entertain people and express his opinions?

I fought with Rina, but she stood by me stoically through the mountains of complaints to the BCCSA that arrived on an almost daily basis. She believed I had potential and was prepared to continue to mentor me, even after she left the station. I struggled to find any kind of consistency. Actually, some things can't be fast-tracked – they just need time. I needed to work out who I was, and to grow up (even if I didn't realise it at the time).

The morning show on 702 wasn't a complete disaster, though. The team kept changing and we evolved in imperceptible ways. Thabo Modisane became my engineer and we spent the next 13 years making some great radio together. Alan Ford, David O'Sullivan, Udo Carelse, Katy Katopodis, Noeleen Maholwana-Sangqu, Charl van Niekerk, Edwin Kgasoe and even Yvonne Chaka Chaka, my other mother, were all part of the morning show family over that period.

Dan Moyane was feeling the pressure as station manager and was promoted into a more corporate position. In Dan's stead, Rina appointed Yusuf Abramjee as station manager. Some may call him a hustler, but Yusuf is a tenacious newshound and activist who relentlessly pursues scoops. We were doing a promotion at the Wild Coast Sun when we received the news that disgraced former national cricket captain Hansie Cronje had been killed in a plane accident. Yusuf sprang into action, juggling two cellphones at the speed of a skilled gunfighter readying for a shootout, contacting sources who gave him the details before anyone else even knew Hansie was dead. If he wasn't actually on the scene before anyone else, he'd sure as hell know about it before you and me.

One day in 2001, Yusuf managed to organise a live broadcast of my breakfast show from Pretoria Central Prison (now Kgosi Mampuru II Correctional Centre) – where Oscar stays from time to time – and it remains a highlight of my time at 702. I remember the smell of prison, sort of sour, like milk that has gone off, the horrendous food – a kind of slop, with a smell of too much yeast and too little care. It was distressing to see the awaiting-trial section, where inmates had to rotate one bed between three or four of them, taking it in shifts to sleep. They even took us on a tour of C-Max, where the most dangerous cons were kept, in cells made entirely of concrete – even the loo was concreted into the floor and wall of the cell. We looked in on Collen Chauke, Moses Sithole and Eugene de Kock, three of SA's most notorious criminals. I remember it was shortly after 9/11, and Chauke had a poster of Osama bin Laden on his wall. C-Max prisoners get let out into the sun for one hour, twice a day – into barbed-wire cages with a cold concrete floor. After that trip, I sincerely hope I never end up in prison. It's awful, just bloody awful.

Another very special memory that year was when I handed a cheque to Nelson Mandela for the cause closest to his heart. When he was diagnosed with prostate cancer, we undertook to create the world's largest 'Get Well Madiba' fresh flower bouquet to raise funds for the Nelson Mandela Children's Fund. Our PR manager, the late Ilana Surat, ably assisted by Aki Anastasiou, swung into action and Sandton City's Fountain Court became a fragrant, glorious floral tribute, where each person bought a flower to add to the bouquet. Several hours later, at 6.5 m in height and 3.75 m in width, and weighing close to four tonnes, our bouquet made it into the *Guinness Book of Records* and a handsome sum was raised. Sadly, Ilana, who taught me all the Yiddish I know and was regarded as the heart of 702, was already undergoing chemotherapy and passed away a few years later. Aki remains one of the longest-standing staff members at 702, still famous for his traffic reports but also establishing himself as one of South Africa's foremost tech journalists.

Despite the challenges of being the youngest talk show host in South African history, my time at 702 introduced me to many wonderful characters – and all of them helped me along the way.

From the outset, Rina engaged the services of Valerie Geller, a world-renowned talk radio consultant based in New York. While the Primedia executives were convinced Rina had made a mistake with me, it was Valerie who lent support. I may not have appreciated it at the time, but I am deeply indebted to Valerie for the wisdom she shared with us in creating powerful radio. She has remained an advisor and a friend to this day.

During my second year on the breakfast show, the chief operating officer (COO) of Primedia, Peter Matlare, moved to become the CEO of the SABC and Rina also left 702, and the two of them began orchestrating my move to 5FM.

It was time to go somewhere I could grow, where I could engage an audience that was dynamic, energetic and had less baggage from our country's complicated past. I needed to talk to people my own age and make a difference in a place where we could define cool. 5FM was that place. Even though I love talking and politics is one of my passions, I equally love music. I was really excited.

Music Radio

Secret negotiations got under way with 5FM, the biggest national youth music station in the country. The plan was that I'd take over the afternoon drive show from Darren Scott and eventually move to mornings, but since SABC contracts ran from April, and it was only November, I had to start off at 6 pm, for three hours every weeknight, until Darren's contract ran out. Alex Jay had been 'retired' from 5FM shortly before, and, unbeknown to Darren, he was next. For me, it meant moving from a prestigious breakfast show to night radio and taking a knock in earnings. That was my first lesson in strategy.

The SABC was completely different to 702. We had studios on the ground floor of the enormous, ugly old building, and the offices were on the eighth floor, past all the security checks. The production studios were underground, in the bowels of the building, where the toilets still had little coloured-in male and female figures for what used to be the black toilets and clear ones for what used to be the white toilets. Some of the people I had always thought were so cool when I was growing up were there – Darren Scott, Sasha Martinengo, Ian F, Barney Simon. I was excited to meet them.

I got a cold reception. Mark Gillman, who was doing the morning show, had instructed everyone not to greet me or make even the slightest overture of friendliness. Really? Here I was, 24 years old, entering a scary new environment, and this guy, who had been on air for several years without an increase in ratings, was telling people to ignore me. I once thought he was tremendously talented, that he had some really original ideas, but it was more of that performance stuff that I felt had become dated. Everyone who knows him well says he's highly intelligent and has a great sense of humour. What a pity we never managed to hit it off. We might have worked well together under different circumstances. That happens in life.

There was one person I needed to join me: Thabo Modisane. Thabo was my technical producer at 702, and was always the voice of calm. He decided to jump ship from 702 and join me as my producer. Finally I felt like I could begin building a team. I inherited Leigh-Ann Mol from Darren Scott's drive show, where she read the news. She had been treated like a lot of women are treated on air in radio – like a bimbo. She didn't like me in the beginning at all … I could tell. Despite excellent credentials as an experienced newsreader and journalist, she couldn't read one news story without screwing it up. I wanted her replaced. Management refused. That was the only thing management ever did that I disagreed with, and I now see it in retrospect as a wise decision. I grew to love Leigh-Ann. She was witty, smart and didn't mind going where others feared to go – even if it meant admitting embarrassing personal hygiene problems with only the slightest provocation.

Thabo was the technical producer, but we needed someone who could help with the content on the show. It had to be someone who understood me like Thabo did, or they'd never last. Thabo was reliable; he was my litmus test for whether things were working or not on the show. If he smiled or laughed, I was on track; if he scowled, I knew I needed to get out. Finding a producer is much harder than finding someone who wants to be on air – producers tend to be a lot less noisy and obvious – but I knew a guy who was, let's just say, *different*: Damon Kalvari.

Damon had also worked with us at 702 and had ended up being fired twice from there. He was a 30-something virgin, still living with his aging parents, and was single until he met Bernice, his equally crazy wife. You know how they say genius and lunatic are next-door neighbours? We never quite figured out whether Damon is more like Larry David (the creator of *Seinfeld*) or the Unabomber. He is the funniest guy I know, and easily the most miserable. He is at once pessimistic, paranoid, filled with self-doubt and obsessive about detail, and then a moment later he's hysterical, wise, objective and perceptive.

Now, I always treated Damon like the whipping boy because he needed to be kept to heel, but he deserves this praise: Damon is a radio expert. If his mouth could only work in tandem with his brain, there would be nothing he couldn't do. He would probably do a better show than me. Despite everything we say about him, our show would have been much less interesting without Damon.

Mabale Moloi joined us when we moved to the breakfast show. We introduced traffic reports to 5FM for the first time, and that was our excuse to get Mabale on air. From studying Medical Microbiology at the University of KwaZulu-Natal, Mabale went from biologist to 'trafficologist', much to the horror of her father. She was a caller to my afternoon show who stood out from that first call. There was something she just 'got' about me, and about the show. Mabale is the listener in the studio, and she does what very few people in radio can do – she listens. While she'll often disagree, and has an infectious laugh, her role is so unique that it complements all the craziness or opinion I'm used to putting out.

Jen Su was our Hollywood reporter, and I always joke that her parents were on the last sampan out of Kowloon. Although born in America, Jen became known on television and radio in Bangkok and Hong Kong, where her husband was marketing director for a large multinational. When I met Jen, her husband had just been transferred to South Africa and she had to start over again. We launched 'The Hollywood Report' on my show on 5FM and it didn't take long for Jen to become South Africa's number-one A-lister herself. She has even written a book on how it's done. Jen somehow manages to attend every social event, not only across the country but also across the planet.

The only role that kept changing, almost annually, was that of the sports anchor. Bo Moseneke (ironically the brother of my 702 producer, Dudu, and son of former Deputy Chief Justice Dikgang Moseneke) was a bright young star, who was taken from us much too soon. Bo died in 2005 due to complications from diabetes, and his beautiful funeral was a real celebration of his short, energetic life. Tony Ndoro was our sports coach for a while and my stand-in whenever I was away, and I've always liked his relaxed, conversational style. Kabelo (KB) Ngakane brought a wild, crazy energy to the studio and needed a show of his own eventually. The final piece of the morning-show puzzle was Sias du Plessis. As crazy as KB was, Sias was sane. What distinguished him even more was that he was ginger, and that he lived a thousand kilometres from work in the deep Free State, which led to hours of fun on air.

5FM Mornings

The afternoon drive show suited me. I enjoyed sleeping late in the mornings and had become a DJ for club events, something I would never have anticipated. In the late 2000s, DJs became a bigger deal than rock stars, and sometimes commanded higher fees. With beautiful girls and drunk people all around, it was an intoxicating and hedonistic alternative to waking up early and doing the morning show. The gigs involved my getting up in front of the crowd, choosing exactly the right music and mixing it all to create the perfect party. It also meant developing a superhuman resistance to shots of tequila.

Those parties kept me in touch with the target market and I don't regret one minute of it, despite the constant travel, constant attention and occasional exhaustion. For about ten years I hardly spent an entire weekend at home. By the time I was ready to leave 5FM, I was also ready to stop playing at the clubs. I didn't want to be that old guy on the decks, trying to entertain people half my age.

Back at 5FM, rumours began circulating about DJ Fresh joining us. It was assumed he would take over from Mark Gillman on the breakfast show, and I was content to keep growing the afternoon show's ratings.

While I was still at 702, I had interviewed DJ Fresh (Thato Sikwane), who was hosting YFM's morning show at the time, and we found much common ground. We had a few discussions about how we could take radio into the next ten or twenty years together. Fresh had a great sense of humour, the best laugh in the world and a good idea of what was hot and happening. We also appeared together on Phat Joe's TV show, just before the move to 5FM, and without any rehearsal or warning we tied Joe up, taped his big mouth shut and took over the show. Nobody expected that, but because it was a live show there was nothing they could do about it. The cameras kept rolling and Fresh and I went crazy. People loved it, and we knew we could give them more.

As it happened, DJ Fresh joined 5FM a few years after I did, and it was during the next seven years, when I was on morning drive and Fresh on afternoon drive, that 5FM enjoyed the most success. When he joined, we wrestled each other in giant sumo suits to determine who would get mornings and who would get afternoons. I won. Fresh will tell you he won. That's bullshit. Ask executive producer Thabo Modisane.

With the move to mornings, in 2007, I updated my Facebook profile: 'Gareth Cliff is a tall, blue-eyed man from Pretoria, the capital city of South Africa. His ancestors oppressed many people over their 300–400 year tenure in Africa. Gareth intends to remedy this with a terrific radio show. 5FM Mornings, Gareth's radio show is on from 6h00–9h00 in the mornings, every weekday on 5FM (not Umhlobo-Wenene, as is often thought). While the hard-working people of Johannesburg, Cape Town, Durban, Polokwane, Bloemfontein and all the other cities (even Port Elizabeth) head off to work early every morning, we keep them company. We spread cheer, information and ribald humour, often upsetting a few old ladies and occasionally upsetting the government.'

The scene was set. I hated waking up so early in the morning but I loved the show. 'You'll get used to it,' people would tell me. You never get used to waking up *that* early; you just get used to how it feels to be up at that time.

Perhaps the most unusual hallmark of my move to 5FM Mornings was having customised jingles recorded by the now-very-famous Soweto Gospel Choir. The co-founder and director, Bev Bryer, had been commissioned to form a grassroots gospel choir to tour Australia. Their first tour was hugely successful but no one at home had ever heard of them. Their South African debut was on my show singing 'Wake up, Wake up with Gareth Cliff' and the famous 'Thabo Modisane Executive Producer' jingle. They went on to win numerous awards, including three Grammy Awards, and have performed across the planet accompanying some of the best-known artists. They have also been the highlight of our annual Cliffmas Carols concert, a fundraiser for Headway Gauteng.

I became involved with Headway Gauteng when I did a favour for a friend and attended their end-of-year party. I was a reluctant guest, preferring not to face such misfortune in other people, but it proved to be a moving experience. They subsequently asked me to be their patron, which I've been ever since. Headway is an inspiring non-profit organisation that looks after people who have suffered brain injuries. These are people who were living normal productive lives and, in a split second, through some unfortunate incident, sustained head injuries that changed their lives forever. I've been lucky enough to walk away from several car accidents with a couple of scratches, as I'm sure you may have too. I also feel embarrassed when the people at Headway thank me for my involvement; the negligible things I have done cannot compare to the sense of mission, generosity and selflessness that I have witnessed not only in those injured, but also in their families, the staff and volunteers. I have felt my life profoundly improved, and my sense of perspective and awareness immeasurably raised, through this experience.

My audience grew and diversified year on year and SABC reaped the benefits in increased revenue. We had started influencing popular culture, and our phrases like 'It's the Weekeeeeeeend Baby' and 'Phuza Thursday' became part of everyday vocabulary. We invented drinking games that the President referred to in his State of the Nation speech, and I believe our team was the best team in radio anywhere. Every morning we'd talk about the news like real people, break the rules, take 'phone calls … we get your phone calls' and play great music.

Social media was a young and exciting new plaything and a great way for us to connect with our audience. Our commercial breaks were sold out and clients loved the stuff we did for their brands. We calculated that the SABC made hundreds of thousands of rands *every day* just from our show. We talked about the stuff people really cared about. Management was like a revolving door right across the SABC and we never knew what would happen in the next year but life was good, even though we lived from year to year … contract to contract.

Contract – Means Not to Expand

At the beginning of every year, contract season began at the SABC. Just like in a marriage, they say that contracts are only there for the bad times. With most employment contracts you have to take it or leave it. What's there to negotiate? You know what I'm talking about. With *Idols* the only thing was checking availability and making travel arrangements. M-Net was always very lax about signing contracts. Until season 12, I only ever signed a contract halfway into an *Idols* season.

At 5FM, my contract was also only ever for a year at a time. We signed in March and then we worked until the following March, when they decided either to get rid of us or to hire us again. After a few years of this, you got used to it and the contract negotiation (which is more like an ultimatum) became fairly routine. Unfortunately at 5FM, we had no choice …

Management always try to find things to complain about at contract meetings so they can avoid paying you a big increase, even though you may have excelled in doing your job and in growing the audience and revenue significantly. They always come up with some left-field reason why they want you to know they could replace you very easily and kick you out there and then. The reality is that they can, and they don't even need a good reason. In the history of radio, talent and success in ratings seldom mean job security, even for the best people in the business. You could deliver everything and more than they ask for and find yourself begging for a show on some unknown community station just because someone didn't like you. It's a cutthroat industry.

When I first joined 5FM, my fellow *Idols* judge Randall Abrahams was the general manager, John Langford, later of Big Concerts fame, was station manager and Nick Grubb, currently the chief executive of radio for Kagiso Media, was programme manager. I was initially approached to take over the afternoon drive show from Darren

Scott, who didn't know his number was up. I joined in November and waited in the wings hosting the 6 pm to 9 pm slot until poor Darren got the axe.

When I moved to afternoon drive I tried to negotiate a commensurate fee. John sent a very long, boring email and said, 'After laughing hysterically, we gave it some serious thought ... blah blah blah ...' Can you imagine your manager laughing at you after you ask for a raise? That's radio for you. Rina replied, realising there was no option, but pointed out the rather lean working conditions for freelancers at the SABC, with absolutely no benefits. That was how it would be for the next ten years.

My own management agreement with Rina was established only a few years after we had been working together. It was one of the few times we consulted a lawyer; in the end, we tossed out all the legalese and wrote our own agreement. The termination clause is that if ever we decide not to work together any longer, we say goodbye with a hug and we don't owe each other anything. It will have all been worth it.

Every year we have a strategy session and every year Rina has pushed me to add something new to my repertoire. You could say that she was actually the one who pushed me 'over the cliff' when I left 5FM. She always said that if you don't constantly up your game, you might as well be treading water, and in order to be independent you have to be your own boss. Then no one can wave a dreaded contract in your face and dictate your salary increase or future.

One day I would have to take my destiny into my own hands, but in the meantime I made negotiation time at 5FM playtime. Each new set of managers brought new ideas in the hope of reinventing the wheel and making a good impression somewhere in the hierarchy. For the most part, I humoured whichever incumbent happened to be in place at the time and accepted the standard 4–6 per cent increase. I always brought my audience in, and we would wonder together at how the meetings would go. Most people can identify with the employment agreement situation and have experienced their own frustrations around this process.

The year before I left, in 2013, my big meeting with management happened to fall on the same day that the cardinals in Rome went into conclave to elect the new Pope. I went on air that morning and explained to my listeners that if the meeting went well, I would release a puff of white smoke from the roof of the SABC building in Auckland Park. If the meeting went badly, the smoke would be black.

Some Catholics thought I was mocking the election of their Supreme Pontiff, which, I can assure you, was the furthest thing from my mind. A woman called Tracey phoned in to tell me that my mockery would not be tolerated. I tried to explain to her that the whole process fascinated me and that I was more excited than most Catholics were by the papal election. She wasn't buying any of it. The reality of the situation was that I was, and remain, engrossed in arcane subjects like the papal conclave, to the degree that my library at home is filled with books on the matter, including one in Latin, printed in the year 1773 and marked '*ex-libris et ex-typographia Clementia XIV*' (from the library and printers of Pope Clement XIV), the same pope who suppressed the Jesuits. Ignorance of the subject is not a valid charge in this case.

On that occasion, my meeting went well and I tweeted a picture at 11 am of really badly photoshopped white smoke coming out of the top of the SABC building. I had signed for another year. *Gaudium magnum! Habemus Papem!*

That was my last contract with 5FM.

Sex, Lies and Newspapers

The part I like least about my job is that, being in the public eye, it's hard to go anywhere incognito. It's almost impossible to go on a regular date, let alone having dinner with a female friend, without it popping up in some or other tabloid as my new love interest. And if it happens to be a male friend, that means I must be gay. I've never understood why anyone would care about who I or anyone else is dating and why the gossip columns continue to thrive. Fortunately only a handful of my relationships were exposed in the press.

While doing afternoons on 5FM, I made a mistake many people make in the workplace: I started developing feelings for a co-worker. I don't like to talk about relationships because I always think the other person should be able to tell their story too, and because I think that when two people share something meaningful it shouldn't be a salacious story for the tabloid press. Just think about Kim Kardashian's stupid 72-day marriage if you need to see what happens when you break this rule.

I started hanging around after my show for longer and longer every night. Nicole Fox was a gorgeous, confident, clever woman, and hosted the evening show on 5FM. I didn't particularly like her radio shows, but she really was very sexy. I remember looking at pictures of her in a magazine, long before we met, and thinking about her naked.

We were invited by *Style* magazine to go to Mauritius to do a review for one of the new resorts there. I loathe seeing couples in magazines doing that kind of thing, with all those posed photographs and cheesy romantic set-ups, but Nicole told me she'd take care of them, and, against my better judgement, I agreed. That was the first and last time I ever posed for photographs with a girlfriend and graced the front cover of a magazine as a couple.

I've since found myself on the front pages of newspapers and magazines more times than I care to count, but have never got used to seeing my face staring back at me from a random newsstand. One front cover that I've been both proud and humbled to be on, though, was for *Destiny* magazine in 2014, when I was photographed with Tim Modise and Bob Mabena for an insert called 'The Evolution of Radio'. These two men are radio giants and people I admired while I was growing up, so it was an honour to be featured alongside them all these years later.

Nicole and I managed to escape any nasty gossip, but a strange thing did happen. While we were away, apparently Mark Pilgrim, who was standing in for me, talked about our relationship on the show. Our relationship was hardly a state secret, but when we got back poor Mark had been fired and the newspapers were all reporting that it was because he had been talking about Nicole and me on the radio, which was ridiculous. All these years later, Pearl Thusi was suspended from Metro FM for talking about Bonang; it seems the more things change, the more they stay the same.

Nevertheless, I don't know whether management did fire Mark for that reason. They had either been looking for a reason to get rid of him (that happens on youth stations when you reach a certain age) or the tabloids were making it up, to be salacious. I was glad he was snapped up by 94.7 and continued with a solid track record. There's no bad blood between us, but if it is in fact true that he was fired for that reason I would be disappointed.

Nicole and I were together for two fantastic years, and I cried like a little puppy when we broke up. We were both building our careers and the personal needs were encroaching. I had to admit early on that, with my career on the rise, I was way too selfish to make the necessary commitment to a relationship, and especially where I really valued a woman; it was only fair to walk away.

Since then I have taken great care to not allow my relationships to become fodder for the tabloids. People love drama. In fact, for generations scandal and gossip have shaped the way we consume newspapers. Do you see how gossip causes trouble, and how stupid the entertainment industry can be? I drive around shaking my head every time I hear a story about how some 'insider' leaked an embarrassing story about a celebrity, or when I hear rumours spread about someone being a diva or an arrogant superstar. People never seem to fabricate nice things about other people. The business is to break people down and make them seem awful. Don't believe everything you read or hear.

I remember watching Larry King talking to Paul Newman on CNN some years back. Paul Newman was one of the greatest Hollywood actors that ever lived, and had one of the longest marriages in the movie business. He and his wife, Joanne Woodward, successfully evaded the rumour mill. Larry asked Newman how he managed this, and he relayed a story of just how twisted this form of journalism can be. He recalled being interviewed about his marriage, and being asked, 'Have you ever beaten your wife?' 'No,' he said, 'of course I've never beaten my wife,' and promptly ended the session, as he could see where it was going. A few days later the interview appeared in the magazine with the headline 'Paul Newman Denies Beating His Wife'.

My run-ins with the press around relationships have been less dramatic than Paul Newman's, but it's so easy to see how things can be misconstrued in the hunt for gossip. I have been extremely protective of my relationships, mostly out of respect for whomever I'm dating. I'm thick-skinned enough to brush off bad press, but relationships are hard enough without the scrutiny of vultures in search of bad news just to make people feel better about their own pathetic lives.

My relationship with Claudia Henkel was also relatively gossip-free, although it was my first experience of photographers hiding in the car park at restaurants where we might be dining. It must be terrible being so famous that paparazzi come out of any conceivable crack in search of the 'money shot', like cockroaches out of a sewer. I met Claudia in a club. I was with a group of friends and across the room, standing at the bar, was the most beautiful woman I had ever seen. I made my move; after dating for a few weeks, she revealed that she was a finalist for Miss South Africa. A few months later she was crowned Miss South Africa and that was the beginning of the end of our relationship. First, Miss South Africa has to forgo having a boyfriend during her year-long reign, and, second, our careers were at an impasse.

Getting involved with an *Idols* contestant also provided the perfect story for the now defunct *Heat* magazine. That was another *Idols* controversy, albeit short-lived; 'Is it ethical for a judge to be dating a contestant?' was the question of the day. As it happened, it was at the *Idols* wrap-up party for Season 6 that Lize and I first locked eyes and later that night ... lips. Technically *Idols* was over – and so was the relationship, a few weeks later. It hadn't been a good idea at all.

And then there was Jeremy Mansfield's seeming obsession about my being gay, which attracted minor media attention. This was an ongoing theme on his very successful morning show on Highveld 94.7. Jeremy was a great broadcaster in his time. I grew up listening to him on the radio and was quite in awe when I first met him. Little did I know at the time that I would be going up against him in the same time slot on 5FM. Maybe he was threatened by this new young upstart on the block. No doubt many people believed him and may wonder to this day whether or not I am gay. Was this meant to put me in a bad light, as though being gay is evil? I wonder.

But my juiciest love story was this one: did you hear about my lover in the North West? If it wasn't for the *Sunday World*, neither would I have! That was my Father's Day surprise – and she was pregnant with my child. Here's what happened ...

Father's Day 2012. What do you buy your dad for Father's Day? It's so much easier to buy for Mother's Day. So I decided that I would have a family breakfast at my house in honour of our Dad. Just some quiet quality family time with my folks, my brother and his wife, my sister and my girlfriend.

Breakfast at my house means quickly running to the shops to buy all the usual breakfast stuff – you know, bacon, eggs, tomatoes. Trolley full and everything on the list ticked off, I headed for the till. The cashier gave me a knowing smile. 'I see you're in the *Sunday World*,' she said. 'Oh,' I said, 'that's nice.' Two months before, I had been arrested for speeding and, as luck would have it for eNCA, they had a reporter cruising with the Metro cops that night in the hope of a story. They bagged me. Unbeknown to me at the time, the entire incident was filmed, and endlessly flashed across the TV screens for days after. What now?

I pulled into the garage shop on my way home and the petrol attendants were pointing and giggling. Now I was very worried. There, on the front page of one of the biggest Sunday newspapers in South Africa, was the headline story, 'Gareth's Black Babe', with a picture of me superimposed with a woman from the North West I had never seen before. The line below the headline read: 'Lovebirds: Miemie Seleka is expecting *Idols* judge Gareth Cliff's baby'. The story continued on page 3 with the headline, 'Gareth smitten with bundu girl – stage set for his little idol'.

I smiled, and my heart started to slow to a normal rate. I suppose I should have been angry or annoyed, but I was just relieved that it was such obvious nonsense. When I got into the car, I read the whole story again. It turned out that a girl called Miemie Seleka from Mahikeng was in an ongoing relationship with me and was pregnant with my 'love child'. All of this was as much news to me as it would have been to any other *Sunday World* reader.

I thought the whole thing really was very funny and was prepared to let it slide, but my girlfriend, Emma Sadleir, found it less amusing.

Emma is a media lawyer and felt the article should be used to highlight the problems with poor journalism, spurious rumour and a dearth of good fact-checking in the print media.

I wrote a letter to the press ombudsman and spoke to my friend Mondli Makhanya, then group editor of the Avusa (now Times Media) papers. He was appalled at the manufacture of such a story out of thin air. It appeared the journalist had gone to print with only hearsay and a steaming pile of bullshit as his sources for this front-page scoop. Although my story was no big deal and did no damage, it opened a can of worms about just how much of the other stuff we read and take as the gospel truth in our supposed news media might be made up. How do you know whom to believe? The following Sunday I got a full front-page apology from the *Sunday World*. I have no idea what became of the journalist in question.

In a world increasingly turning to the internet for the latest news, the old procedures and rules adhered to by competent journalists have been superseded by a need for speed and sensation over any degree of truth or veracity. While most of us now hear about breaking stories from Twitter, Facebook, online news tickers or apps on our smart-phones, we still have to be careful whom and what we trust as credible sources for information that might, in some circumstances, be a matter of life and death.

My heart goes out to all those victims of wiretapping and phone hacking in Britain. Thanks to Rupert Murdoch's scurrilous minions, people who had lost loved ones in war and tragedy found their private thoughts and most intimate words copied and pasted on the front pages of tabloid rags. The 'journalist' has split into two distinct sub-species: the first is a reporter who checks all his or her facts and sometimes breaks the least sexy story because it is important to do so, because it is something we need to know. The other is the kind of slovenly blogger-cum-celebrity stalker whose only goal is to sell sensational copy today.

While my story doesn't illustrate the very worst in journalism, it does show up the low standard that most publications seem inclined to accept – because it is cheap and because it requires no skill – on even the front pages of their most valuable assets. They're throwing away the only thing that will make their business viable online – credibility.

I have never heard from my 'girlfriend' Miemie or my supposed baby, who must have been born in the interim, so I can only hope they're both well.

I won't be answering any calls on Father's Day for the next few years, just in case.

Hollywood

My time at 5FM did have some unusual perks, some of which took me to exotic destinations. I took a trip to the USA in 2004 that gave me an opportunity to look Hollywood squarely in the eye. I was flown first class to Los Angeles by Virgin Atlantic to attend the Oscars, an NBA All-Star game and fit in a quick visit to New York. I sat next to Boris Becker on the way to LA from London – and he asked a lot of questions about black women in Africa.

Once in LA I got to meet a bunch of famous people – we really did have access to things someone like me should never have. Now I don't want to sound like that annoying name-dropping Piers Morgan, but on the first day I got to meet basketball legends Shaquille O'Neal (the biggest man I have ever seen – he could have stopped the white man's oppression all on his own), Yao Ming (so tall that you could fold him in half and he'd still bump his head on the top of a door-frame) and Kareem Abdul-Jabbar (who I thought was a bastard for telling a kid to f**k off when he asked for an autograph). I knew nothing about basketball and I felt like a dwarf. People don't like to talk about this, but when someone is much taller than you, your default reaction is to hate them and become hostile. I feel so sorry for all those short people I must have upset for most of my adult life. I had to go all the way to America to discover this bit of life-changing wisdom.

I attended a breakfast with Madeleine Albright, who was Secretary of State under President Bill Clinton. She spoke about terrorism and America's place in the world, and I asked her about ten questions. Although she looked like Yoda from *Star Wars* and had less hair on her head than Homer Simpson, I think it was important for a former International Relations student to have had the chance to spend an hour or two in the company of the woman who was determining the course of international relations at the very time I was studying the subject. It all felt very satisfying, and I thought I was very important – until I was nearly run over by a cab while walking to my next destination.

We went to the Staples Centre to see some of the rehearsals for the NBA All-Star game. Bear in mind that up to this point the most famous artists I'd seen perform were Mango Groove. It was midday, and hardly anyone was in the arena. From the stage I heard a song I thought I knew: 'Well it's been building up inside of me for oh, I don't know how long ...' The Beach Boys were warming up and doing a sound check. *The fucking Beach Boys!* I walked right up to the stage, so close I could see Brian Wilson's ADHD snap on and off, and sat down on the floor. I didn't leave until after the game, at 11 pm. I got to watch, with an audience of disinterested labourers, the likes of Michael McDonald, Nelly Furtado and Christina Aguilera. When they opened up for the game, the whole place filled up with celebrities. I had an all-access pass, and so I walked around like I was important. Jack Nicholson was sitting courtside, and I went right over and said hello. He brushed me off and said, 'Yeah, okay.' I told him I was a huge fan of his work and he just looked at me with utter revulsion. 'No photographs, and no autographs, okay?' All I have to remind me of my encounter with one of the greatest actors of all time is a stupid photo of me jumping into the frame behind a grimacing Jack Nicholson. If he had been nice, I'd have been disappointed. I like Jack all crabby and grumpy.

Photobombing Jack Nicholson, NBA All-Star game, 2004.

I saw an unoccupied seat right next to P-Diddy and took it. Until they throw me out, I thought, I'll stay right here. Diddy thought I was someone important and said hello to me. I was in! Heather Locklear was sitting a few seats down, with Chris Tucker, Ashton Kutcher, Will Smith, Magic Johnson and Kirsten Dunst. I'm not going to give you the laundry list, but it was funny when Dr Phil sat down and the crowd booed him. If you've ever been to an NBA All-Star game, you'll know the following, but if you haven't, this might interest you:

The whole game is a spectacle. You have two all-star teams (representing the Eastern and Western Conferences) who play a really fast, action-packed game of basketball against each other. You don't have a second to get bored, because every time the action stops, the Kiss Cam zooms in on some celebrity couple who have to kiss and get applause in return. It's a whole production, with music, lights and fireworks.

I had a rude awakening when a fat African-American woman I would later discover was Star Jones came to claim her seat from me. I got out of there fast, because she had a tattooed boyfriend to back her up if I resisted, and she was frightening enough on her own. I did laugh to myself when, at halftime, the cameras zoomed in on Star and her trashy boyfriend as he knelt down and proposed to her. Could have been me making that proposal, Star ...

That night I went to sleep thinking about Los Angeles, and how everyone there was scratching and clawing their way to fame. If you met them in the street, with all the bling and the fancy cars and shopping bags, you'd think there was nobody poor in that town. In my experience, the real LA is a soulless place, where paint peels off the façades and great big highways crisscross a barren, sweltering wasteland of unrealised dreams. Heavy shit, huh?

Enough about that parking lot called Los Angeles. New York is my favourite city in the world – and that's where I was going. On the flight I got to sit next to a proper, dinkum rocket scientist, and he told me he was designing a probe set to explore Io, one of the moons of Jupiter. I was delighted, because usually I end up sitting next to disgusting or boring people on planes. We talked for much of the way. If you've ever flown on Delta or American Airlines, you might have noticed the cabin crew are really old. They're so old that when they pass you with the trolley, dust comes off of them and settles on your lap. I think we retire ours before they start looking like walnuts, just as well ... When we landed, some lady from the West Coast was taking a long time to get her stuff and held everyone up. A New Yorker started yelling at her. I love New Yorkers. They hate wasting time and don't take anyone's nonsense.

New York is the centre of the universe. I've been there almost ten times since and it's the only place I've ever been where I know for sure I could live outside of South Africa. There's such an energy that you only need a few hours' sleep to function properly. It feels like even the smallest occurrence in New York could have an immediate effect globally.

The first time I flew to New York, I landed at JFK International Airport feeling like a homeless person had taken a shit inside my head. I suffer occasional migraines; I've had them since the latter part of high school and they're totally debilitating. I have no idea when a migraine is going to strike or why, but it turns me into a shaking, senseless disaster. I can't speak, I go numb all over my face, I lose feeling in my hands and I start seeing everything in patchy, out-of-focus standard definition. If you know someone who gets migraines, tell them to write stuff down or record them talking when they're going through it. It's exactly the same language those charlatans in charismatic churches call 'speaking in tongues' – just a monstrous, messy, mellifluous word salad. On the plane to New York back in 2000, I got one of these.

By the time we reached the terminal it had started wearing off, but I was still fragile. We took a cab along the Long Island Expressway and the driver was a Senegalese man who intermittently hit the brakes, sending me rocking forward and backward until I was so nauseous I had to concentrate hard not to throw up all over his stinking cab. By the time I reached my hotel room, I was pale and weak and miserable, so I thought I'd have a shower and go straight to sleep. When I got out of the shower I opened the window and looked up Seventh Avenue to Central Park, and down the same street to Times Square. There was no way I could sleep. I put on a pair of trainers and a baseball cap, and grabbed some headphones and went out into Midtown Manhattan, where everything I saw or that happened to me felt like it was part of a movie. In fact, Madonna did jog past me up in Central Park, with a giant bodyguard wheezing while he tried to keep up, so I might as well have been in a movie. Beyond that, I can't account for my time while I was in NYC. I know I did a lot of walking.

I had to fly back to LA to attend the Oscars with Randall Abrahams (who was already my co-judge on *Idols*) and Azania (from Metro FM). The flight back was like the glimpse of hell Dante gives us in the *Inferno*. I'm still traumatised, so I don't really want to talk about it, but a large, unkempt woman sat next to me and opened an eating factory of sardines, bread, cream cheese, liver paté and a smorgasbord of other stinking food. She was probably Oprah's actual eating teacher.

Hollywood is so fake. Everyone air-kisses and tries to look good, but the Oscars really show you what bullshit the whole movie business is. Here you have this massive industry of actors, people who pretend for a living, that gather many hundreds of times a year to congratulate themselves on having pretended better than the other waiters who want to pretend full-time. The Oscars are at the top of this rancid garbage-heap of ego-feeding, ass-licking and self-aggrandising backslapping. The Kodak Theatre (now the Dolby Theatre) on Hollywood Boulevard is in the middle of a neighbourhood that looks like Germiston. On the big day, all the places that are about to appear on TV get dressed up with red carpets, expensive fabrics, statues, plants in pots, a fresh coat of paint and scaffolding. Joan Rivers and her nest of vipers took up their places in the approach and tore precocious young actresses apart for a hemline that's so high the world could be your gynaecologist. Ryan Seacrest asks the most banal, uninteresting vanilla questions he can think up and everyone starts pouring in. We weren't important enough to take part in any of that, but I did get the inside track ... from Tim Robbins.

We were staying in a very fancy hotel called L'Ermitage, in Beverly

Hills. They had a fantastic spa on the roof where a tough Asian woman would give you a tortuous massage, and where you could wallow like a hippo in the pool or sweat like a pig in the sauna. I elected the latter and had just started to settle in when the man nominated for a Best Supporting Actor Oscar (for *Mystic River*) walked in. What a terrific down-to-earth guy he was. I told him how much I had admired his work in *The Shawshank Redemption*, and almost started becoming an irritating fan when he asked me where I was from. Turned out he was headed to South Africa a month or two later and needed to learn some of the peculiarities of our accents. What a stroke of luck that I could finally be useful to someone truly famous. I must have spent a good 20 minutes listening to his stories and telling him how to sound like white trash from Benoni when, appropriately, he brought up Charlize Theron. She was up for the Best Actress award that year and was the talk of the town. Actually, one of the reasons we got such VIP treatment is because of the Charlize connection.

The night of the Oscars was a bit of a blur. I don't remember the details but I know we were thrilled about Charlize's win. We screamed like the murder victims in *Monster* when she went up to get her award and the rest is a muddle. The focus, really, is on the afterparties – because actors all have substance-abuse problems and can't sit through that ceremony without the promise of drugs and liquor and arse-kissing afterwards. Well, we went to two or three parties – I really don't remember – but when we got back to the hotel it was 3 am. Nobody was tired; we were ebullient, and drunk. I offered to get yet more drinks from the bar and sidled up next to an attractive woman with dark red hair, but didn't bother to look at her much; I was completely celebrity-saturated (something which I am grateful to have remained ever since). Or so I thought …

Now I don't mind if you think I'm talking unadulterated, fabricated, concocted horseshit, but here's what happened: I ordered a vodka and lime for Azania, a whisky for Randall and a vodka and Red Bull for myself. This hot woman turned her head, looked me up and down and asked where I was from. 'South Africa,' I said matter-of-factly. She leaned in and kissed me, full on the lips. Before the kiss was even over I felt like someone had set my balls on fire. It was Julianne Moore. She said nothing more, got up and walked away before I could even figure out what had happened. Damn, I thought, she must have been drunk. The only way a woman like that would kiss me was if Bill Cosby had got to her first. I know you think I'm making this up, but I have witnesses, and I'm not mad – and fuck you for being such a doubting Thomas.

I'm not going to tell you any more about America, because after the Julianne Moore story, everything else sounds lame and limp and listless. Let's just hold that vision – my 15 seconds of real fame – being smooched by Julianne Moore.

Party Like a Rock Star

It wasn't quite as sexy, but I had another brush with famous people in mid-2004 when I hosted the Cokefest in Durban. Now that name may sound like a drug-fuelled orgy, but was in fact a massive rock concert sponsored by Coca-Cola and featuring the bands Metallica, Collective Soul and a host of local musicians. It was held in King's Park Stadium to a sell-out crowd and I was excited to see some real rock stars up close. Let me skip right to the fun part.

A girlfriend at the time who was living in Durban came to the show with me. She'll remain nameless to protect her reputation, and because she remains a great friend. The concert was loud and fantastic, and afterwards I was tasked with the job of finding a venue for an afterparty. Since the concert was held on a public holiday, nothing was open – not a bar, not a nightclub, not a restaurant. It was also pretty late.

This girlfriend and I tried everywhere, and we called all the contacts we had in Durban, to no avail. I started to think we'd have to send Lars Ulrich or Ed Roland to bed without a party befitting their rock-star street cred. As a last-ditch plan, I called the promoter and told him we'd make it happen at the Hilton Hotel bar. My girlfriend called up all her hottest mates, and I called a few of my wild friends and commanded them to be present. Some tried to weasel their way out with excuses about having work the next day or wanting a quiet night in, but I insisted. We couldn't have Metallica or Collective Soul go home bored. Durban's (and South Africa's) reputation was at stake. I asked the promoter (who was my old station manager, John Langford) to trust me to get the bar open and to open a tab for some tequila. To his credit, John did.

When we got to the hotel, the bar was shut up and dead quiet. It was like a mausoleum. Even the lady at the front desk was lying sleeping on her arms. Jazz music played softly to an empty lobby and the next day's newspapers lay on a coffee table waiting to be read by over-eager early risers. I was worried that this was going to be a disaster. Full of bravado, I called the hotel manager at home and insisted that we make this happen. These were BIG celebrity rock stars. Everyone was on their way. We turned on lights, opened doors, opened the bar, put on some music and turned the place into an instant carnival. Thank goodness enough of our friends arrived to make it look like a party, and by the time the bands got there with their people it was rocking.

Before long the music was at full volume, a lot of people ended up in the pool, and it went from an old ladies' tea party to bedlam. Girls were dancing on the bar, clothes were shed and I found myself partying with Rock Gods. Ed Roland, who had been on my show the previous year, remembered and gave me his number. That's not just politeness, is it? I think I arm-wrestled a big security guard and lost a bet because I remember waking up with a sore hand, and Collective Soul's manager laughed at me when I next saw him at the airport. We ended up heading to the hotel rooms around 4 am. Secretly, I was very pleased with the havoc we caused at the bar.

The next morning was horrible. I woke up disgustingly hung over, and felt like a vulture had attacked the back of my throat. My girlfriend, who had been in the bed when I passed out, was nowhere to be found. I knew I had an early flight back to Johannesburg to do my show that afternoon. Ugh. I fell back on the pillow and decided to cash out. I needed to recover, so I hit upon the idea of cancelling my show and flying later in the day. I picked up the phone and called the radio station, telling them I needed a stand-in.

News travels fast, and not 20 minutes later Rina called. 'I hear you're not doing your show today. What's going on?' I told her the story. 'If you're not on air this afternoon, you can find yourself a new manager. You're such a big deal, partying like a rock star – and now you're going to just wimp out like a weasel. Man up and get your butt to work.' She put the phone down. I leapt out of bed and into the shower, resentful, chided and suffering with a god-awful headache. I got to the airport in time, but only by a ball-hair.

Suddenly I thought of my girlfriend. Where the hell had she gone? Maybe she was already back at her house or at work. I called her. The phone just rang. You know how you always leap to the most dreadful conclusions when someone can't be reached? I thought she'd fallen over the balcony, driven home drunk or been abducted. I called again. This time she answered, but she was whispering. 'Are you okay?' I asked. 'Yeah,' she said, 'but I'm in his room, and my clothes are in your room. Can you get them to me?' The 'he' in question was a famous musician, and I told her I was at the airport already. She just giggled nervously. I understand that she ran down three flights of stairs and through a few busy corridors of the hotel in a bathrobe to get her clothes and her reputation back.

The moral of the story is that if you want to party with real rock stars, you better be prepared to work like one. Always show up.

Desperate Times Call for Desperate Measures

You may think that my line of work is always filled with exotic travel, fancy parties, champagne and gorgeous girls. It isn't. I have hosted a few concerts and so manage to go backstage and hang with the VIPs, and sometimes you see and hear interesting things. The rest of the time, my life is pretty ordinary. I mentioned before how much I dislike traffic, and I'm sure you too have sat in gridlock and fantasised about cars that could fly. I would love to have my own private helicopter and avoid the traffic – in my dreams.

I really like helicopters. A lot. The best feeling I've ever had with my clothes on was taking the controls of a little Bell helicopter between Cape Town airport and Hermanus. The pilot only let me handle the cyclical – that little joystick that moves the helicopter up down, left and right. Just doing that, you have complete control over all the dimensions, and you feel weightless. The bubble of the cockpit shows the ground flying past underneath; above the clouds and to the left and right is the sky the way a bird sees it. What a tremendous sense of motion and freedom.

I have only once made a grand entrance in a helicopter, and it wasn't as glamorous as it might sound. In December 2010, I was booked to host a concert in Knysna called Knysna Rocks. It was a cool line-up of top local bands, with a sell-out crowd of holiday-makers who flock to that part of the world for the Christmas season. The event was on from three in the afternoon until late, so I had a 9 am flight booked from Joburg to George, giving me ample time to take a leisurely drive from George to Knysna and settle in before the show. This has to be one of the most beautiful parts of South Africa – you don't want to be in a rush when you're taking in the beauty of the Southern Cape.

The problem was, it was between Christmas and New Year and I had thrown a big house party the night before. I slept through the alarm (nothing unusual about that) and woke up with a start a short while later, realising that I had a plane to catch and it wasn't going to wait for me. After a mad dash to the airport, I reached the boarding gate with my ticket just after boarding closed. I could see the plane waiting on the tarmac a few metres away. But no amount of begging or pleading would change the mind of the guy at the gate. Damn. I turned round and walked back, defeated.

Now, I rather pride myself on never missing a booking or an engagement – with one or two unavoidable exceptions. I couldn't let these people in Knysna down. The problem with the Garden Route is that there aren't a lot of flights down there, and driving from Cape Town takes five to six hours. I had to make a plan. Since I had missed my flight by only a minute, I ran around the airport trying to get on the next flight. The only flights were after 4 pm, which would have made me three hours late at a minimum.

Bags in hand, looking the worse for wear, I went to those counters where the really rich people charter jets. Even they weren't able to help me. Eventually I found a low-cost airline that had a seat free on the 2 pm flight. That would mean we would land at George at 3.30 pm and I could make it to the gig by 4.30 pm – only an hour late. Feeling somewhat relieved, I booked the ticket and called the concert organisers to tell them the plan. They sounded very disappointed: the main act was going on stage at 4 pm and that's when they needed me.

My own stupidity had got me into this mess. It's one thing to let yourself down, but when you're booked months in advance to host a concert for a packed crowd, you let others down and do your reputation damage in the process. I came up with a plan: I'd charter a helicopter.

But would they have helicopters in George? You don't exactly think of George as a thriving metropolis where folk commute by helicopter. But if I could go by helicopter to Knysna from George, it would take 20 minutes and I'd make the show. It took a few calls and the plan rolled into action.

Thankfully the flight was on time. When we landed in George, I leapt off the plane to be met by a man in a suit who took my bags and escorted me straight to the helicopter. From the sweaty shameful wreck of a few hours earlier, I now felt like Jack Bauer in an episode of 24. We took off for Knysna and landed in the middle of a field, right next to the crowd. For a minute I could imagine how real celebrities feel when they make such a grand entrance. The timing was so perfect that the crowds no doubt thought that this was a stunt devised by the organisers to add a sense of drama and prestige to the start of the concert. Little did they know …

It cost a fortune, and I think we made a loss on the whole gig, but it was worth every cent. Not only did I get that helicopter ride but I also kept my record and reputation safe. I also had my 15 minutes of feeling what it must be like to be so famous that you arrive on cue in a grand helicopter.

Meeting Bieber

Talking about helicopters and rock stars, my other near-famous experience was when I almost met Justin Bieber. They say that the biggest event in South African concert history was the Justin Bieber concert in Johannesburg in May 2013. Bigger than Michael Jackson. The hype around this guy is ridiculous. He has one of the biggest Twitter followings in the world, sells millions of albums, has fanatical, crazy, lunatic fans who will do anything to meet him or just be near him. People compare the Belieber phenomenon to the Beatlemania of the 1960s and I get the comparison. It's crazy.

I was considering turning down the invitation to go to the concert. There is a particular pitch that excited screaming teenage girls reach, and the thought of a stadium full of them all screaming at once was a little daunting. I was even invited to the meet and greet with Justin, which cost others something to the tune of R5 000 per photograph, but that didn't swing it. But then I got an offer I couldn't refuse. A group of women had hired a helicopter to go to the concert as a birthday surprise for one of their friends. Nice friends, I thought. I should have friends like that. My friends just buy me shitty gifts from the Crazy Store for my birthday. Anyway, there was a spare seat so they asked me if I wanted a ride. Hell yes! You know how much I love helicopters.

We arrived at Grand Central Airport, just outside Pretoria, at 4 pm on that Sunday afternoon, and 45 minutes later boarded the helicopter. I sat up front with the pilot. We got to see a brilliant highveld sunset lighting up the golden calabash that is the FNB Stadium. The sun was setting as we approached, and we could see the crowd starting to mass. Some of them had been camped outside the stadium for two days.

The helicopter people had applied for clearance to land close to the stadium, but permission was denied by the authorities. They figured that if there was any suspicion that Justin was on board, there would be no stopping the Beliebers storming it and having their heads chopped off by the rotor blades. So for safety reasons we had to land some distance away. We did think it would be fun, though, to pull my hoodie over my head, put on shades and run out of the copter as if I were Justin. Imagine the horror of the fans when they saw it was only me! Instead I dashed in to get to the meet and greet, which was scheduled for 5.30.

I really did want to meet Justin and get a picture, but I was stopped by others wanting photographs with me. I tried to look like I was on a mission, but they were undeterred. Fifteen pictures later I finally found a security guard who pointed me in the right direction and ran, huffing and puffing, down three or four flights of stairs into the basement, where the meet and greet was happening. When I saw Attie van Wyk of Big Concerts, he was in a golf cart with someone. 'Hey, did you make it to the meet and greet?' he called. My heart sank. Oh shit, I thought. I'm too late.

I had more fun watching the people in the stadium. There were two young girls in the suite where I was – Tyra and Jenalee. They must have been about seven or eight. Since they couldn't get to meet Justin, they asked me to pose for a picture with them. I was the consolation prize. I said, 'Let's all pull faces for the picture.' They made funny faces but I didn't. When we looked at the picture I said, 'Look at this – you are pulling faces and you still look better than me!' During the concert they were beside themselves with excitement. They knew every word to every song and sang along with unabashed gusto. When Justin lifted his arm they screamed, he walked and they screamed, he sat and they screamed, he picked up a guitar, took off his jacket, brushed his hair – anything he did, they screamed. You could see this was the best night of their lives. Ever. There was nothing that any human could do that could get them more excited than they were that night. Such adoration. Imagine a few thousand young girls screaming at the same time. All the vuvuzelas in the World Cup couldn't compete.

After the concert I saw the cutest interaction between two girls – one white and one black – who couldn't have been more than six or seven. They were obviously friends at school or somewhere, but had just seen each other after the concert. This was the moment to share their Bieber experience. They both screamed and ran into each other's arms in this perfect embrace of shared joy. It just proved to me how stupid and unimportant these divisions are between us. All that matters is sharing experiences together, creating memories together.

Friendship is about having common interests, being motivated and excited by the same things. It was that moment of simple euphoria that made those two little girls represent exactly what was good about human beings. To my mind they looked like the most perfect friends. If Bieber was in that crowd and had to take anything away, if he knew anything about the country, and if he understood the symbolism of those two girls, he would have been proud. That, to me, was the highlight of the whole evening (beside the helicopter ride, of course).

It's amazing how quickly they de-rig the stadium. By the time we flew over, it was empty – as if nothing had happened there. Little did we know that, deep in the bowels of the stadium, people were hard at work with a pneumatic drill stealing R3 million – the evening's takings from the concession stands. Only in South Africa. Maybe they were drilling every time the girls screamed so no one would have heard. When he got back to America and heard about the heist, Justin tweeted, 'It wasn't me!'

Seeing Johannesburg from the air at night is quite magnificent. During the day you just see the greenery of the trees, but at night they disappear and all you see is gold. The streetlights are golden, the car lights are golden. The city looks like a massive vascular system; the roads become veins carrying golden blood. M1, Oxford Road, Buccleuch interchange – all become veins carrying the golden lifeblood of the city. You don't see any of the ugliness at night. The city looks serene and beautiful and at peace.

I did spare a thought for all those thousands of people fighting their way out of the stadium parking and making the long trek home. It must have taken them hours. I also thought of the excited little girls who, when they eventually did get to bed, wouldn't be able to sleep that night. I got home, climbed into bed and imagined being at the controls of that helicopter.

Losing Vicus

An accidental chapter in my life was the year we found Vicus … and lost him again. For a few months in early 2012 everyone was talking about Vicus, who became known as 'The Bieber from Bloem'. Like Justin Bieber, Vicus was discovered on YouTube. In 2010, a video of a ten-year-old boy singing 'These Arms' by All-4-One appeared on the internet. It attracted attention in America and hundreds of thousands of people viewed the video and predicted that this was the next Michael Jackson. Rumour had it that the boy, known only as Vicus, was either from South America or from somewhere in the Eastern Cape in South Africa.

On any given day I receive a variety of requests for jobs, sponsorships, relationship advice, help with finding lost animals or kids, complaints about the government and parents begging me to listen to their children's demos, just to name a few. One email that did catch my attention was from the A&R director of Def Jam in New York:

Hi Gareth–

My name is Shani Gonzales and I am Vice President of A&R at Island Def Jam and my partner Omar Grant is Vice President of A&R for Sony Music. A few weeks ago, we were down in South Africa looking for Vicus, the little boy playing the guitar on a YouTube posted video. Obviously, we had no luck. I have no idea where we go from here. We thought reaching out to you might help am reaching out because I know you are the most popular and well-loved radio personality in the country.

It's probably a long shot, but perhaps we can discuss partnering up to locate Vicus? I know this is not the most traditional way to locate someone. But then again, nothing about this whole scenario is traditional. 2 Americans coming to South Africa on a whim to locate a boy they found on YouTube. No real leads, no contact, just a spirit of adventure, and knowing that this kid can be huge. :-) You get my drift!

Combined Omar and I have extensive experience and have worked with the best and brightest singer, rappers, bands, producers, and songwriters We are confident that once we locate Vicus, we can move swiftly in providing him the best opportunities, including one to sign at Island Def Jam.

Would love to chat with you whenever you have a moment. All of my details are below or you if want to email me with your number, then I can call you. Whichever is easier. I'm holding onto my blackberry all weekend! So I am ready anytime you are.

Thank you so much!
Shani
Shani Gonzales
Vice President, A&R
Island Def Jam
Worldwide Plaza // 825 Eighth Avenue, 28th floor,
    New York, New York 10019

At the time I hadn't heard of Vicus, but this did catch my attention. After an on-air mention on my show, a Facebook update and a tweet, I received hundreds of replies with rumours of the boy being spotted here, there and everywhere. A fellow radio announcer in Bloemfontein, Eric Says, contacted me on Twitter. He knew the kid, and, lo and behold, Vicus was found!

By now Vicus Visser was 17 years old and living in Heidedal, a suburb of Bloemfontein best known for poverty, crime and drug abuse. A story in the *Daily Sun* two days later revealing Vicus's whereabouts caused the media to descend en masse on his family's little house. Record executives and journalists zeroed in on this overwhelmed young guy with promises of fame and fortune. Rina, having been in the media industry for such a long time, was immediately concerned for his well-being, as well as for that of his family. She flew down to Bloemfontein to meet him, and not only did she discover Vicus but also his talented older brother Vincent; the two of them had been singing together since early childhood.

Mother Elsie and stepfather Fanie lived in a small RDP house and brothers Vicus and Vincent in a tin shack in the yard. Elsie's own story was one of spousal abuse, with the boys' father being a chronic alcoholic. These were the memories Vicus recalled from his formative years. She left with her sons when Vicus was ten, and lived with various friends until she met Fanie. The YouTube clip of Vicus that went viral was recorded during this time by a neighbour, but no one knows who actually uploaded it.

At 17, Vicus still had the same star quality that had been captured on the video. Rina and I agreed to manage him and his brother and 'secured' them for Shani and Omar, as we had set out to do. You don't get better than Sony and Def Jam in America, but the whole thing was a little odd. When the contract arrived, it was issued in the name of a new company called 'Finding Vicus Music' with very little in it for Vicus. While he had his sights set on the world stage, Vicus decided to take things slowly and rather finish school and start his career in South Africa. He seemed very wise for such a young man who had certainly experienced some of the worst life has to offer, and with music being his only refuge and succour.

We secured sponsorship and relocated the brothers to Johannesburg where Vicus would complete matric with a private tutor. A record deal was signed with David Gresham Records and the first original song was recorded and released. *Carte Blanche* aired a special feature and several magazines documented the brothers' inspiring story. Vicus passed matric and both he and Vincent were given bursaries from Boston Media House and were enrolled to study for a diploma starting in 2013. It all seemed like the perfect fairy tale, and they were both poised for big careers in the music industry.

The South African Embassy in Washington, DC, heard about Vicus, and Ambassador Ebrahim Rasool and Deputy Johnny Moloto invited me to bring Vicus and his brother to perform at the John F Kennedy Center for the Performing Arts during Black History Month in February 2013, to honour Madiba and Martin Luther King, Jr. It seemed they were ready to wow the world, and they did. This was not only a once-in-a-lifetime opportunity for these two boys, who only months earlier were living in a tin shack, but it was also a huge honour for me to host the concert at one of the most prestigious venues in the world.

Vicus was now most certainly *found*, and was ready to take on the world. The show, called 'Singing the Dream for South Africa', was to be an hour filled with well-known South African songs and some American freedom songs. *Top Billing* presenter Jonathan Boynton-Lee came with us to Washington to cover the event so that South Africans at home could witness this heartwarming story. It was all a terrific example of living the dream.

It seemed that all the time and effort we put in was worth it. Vicus was set to be the biggest star out of South Africa. Alas, it was not to be. One of the people who expressed an interest in him was a beautiful Ethiopian American woman called Debbie Asrate, who had worked at Black Entertainment Television (BET). She seemed very connected, but we quickly realised that there was more sizzle than substance. The brothers nevertheless spent time with her before flying home; in that short time, she managed to convince them that they could bypass studying and South Africa and immediately claim the American Dream. They were mesmerised.

And so Vicus was lost. The brothers forfeited their places at college by not attending lectures and soon enough found themselves back in Bloemfontein, having given up everything while waiting for Debbie to make the American Dream come true for them. They apparently did spend some months with her in the States, but, sadly, to the best of our knowledge, they've been waiting it out back in Heidedal ever since.

Was it a case of 'too much too soon'? How many stories do we hear where success is so close but the poverty cycle and damage suffered in the formative years is just too great to allow the person to go the distance? I often wonder how damaged young South Africans are, both by our brutal past and by the destruction of the family unit.

Vicus – lost and found ... and lost again. I hope, for his sake, not for ever.

When a Plan Comes Together

Exactly a year later, I was back in New York. It was actually in a cheesecake shop on Seventh Avenue, on 14 February 2014, that my decision to leave 5FM crystallised ... the same day that Oscar Pistorius shot his girlfriend, the beautiful Reeva Steenkamp. Rina and I ordered coffee, and, despite the snowstorm outside and our disbelief about Oscar and Reeva, found ourselves in high spirits. In New York you have to call it 'caaawwfee' or they look at you funny, even if they themselves are from Bratislava.

We were in New York for an auspicious occasion – the first international commemoration of the life of Nelson Mandela, just two months after his death in December 2013. *New York* magazine and the *Wall Street Journal* hailed the tribute as the 'event of the week'.

It had been a beautiful and rarefied experience for the select group of influential New Yorkers who made the trek through the snow to the Church of St Paul the Apostle on the Upper West Side. A major snowstorm overnight had put our entire programme in jeopardy. Actor Morgan Freeman, who was scheduled to read extracts from Madiba's letters and speeches, was stranded across the country and couldn't get a plane into the city. The famous Grammy-award-winning Soweto Gospel Choir was locked down in Washington, DC, with no land or air transport that would brave the storm. Everything was up in the air. I was to be the Master of Ceremonies and President William Jefferson Clinton was to give the eulogy – the first by any world leader since Mandela's funeral in Qunu on 15 December 2013.

I was so nervous. Everything we had planned might have to be changed at the last minute. Without the choir, there might be too much talking, and none of that special African music. Without Morgan Freeman, the event wouldn't have the shine of one of Hollywood's biggest stars. It might be down to Bill Clinton and me. And who knew if he would still make it through the heaviest snowstorm New York had experienced that winter? We started revising the script ...

By the afternoon, the storm had started to clear. Morgan Freeman managed to board one of the few flights that left Los Angeles for New York. Bev Bryer, director of the Soweto Gospel Choir, had been frantically trying every avenue to get the choir from Washington, and eventually persuaded the bus driver to at least attempt the journey and drive very slowly. The four-hour journey took seven hours, but they made it. The Nelson Mandela Foundation's CEO, Sello Hatang, had been very particular about the programme of events, and Madiba's longtime assistant and friend, Zelda la Grange, was there to make sure every detail of protocol and protection of the Mandela legacy was observed. In New York, our friend Pamela Mirels and her company, Culturehorde, coordinated the event and eliminated every possible glitch in what was planned to be a perfect evening.

What an intimate and uplifting affair it turned out to be. There was nothing sombre and pretentious about it. Morgan Freeman even got up and danced during the choir's lively 'Pata Pata'. 'That's what Madiba would have liked,' said Zelda.

The essence of President Clinton's tribute was that if it was possible for Mandela to forgive and reconcile, it might also be possible for us to walk away from even justified anger with another person, especially if they were different. He said that was the problem with the whole world, that people fought because they saw others as different, and because they thought their anger was justified. He said that he had asked Madiba if he hated his jailers, and that he had replied, 'Yes, but only for a few seconds, then I forgave them.' And that Madiba had told him that continuing to hate them would have kept him in prison forever. To be truly free, he had to let go of anger and bitterness.

This was one of the proudest moments of my life. Not only honouring Madiba so appropriately, but also chatting to a former President of the United States, and laughing with one of the greatest actors of our time, in the city I regard as the centre of the universe.

It was a deeply personal, sacred moment of reflection and honour that I still can't believe I played a part in.

RIP Madiba

The passing of Madiba had a profound effect on me – more than I could have anticipated. I had met him a few times. When I was at university I became friendly with his grandson Mandla Mandela; we were both studying International Politics and we used to hang out at the house in Houghton. I went to Mandla's first wedding in Qunu, but since then, while we stay in SMS contact, our paths have diverged, to say the least.

When it comes to death, I'm more philosophical than spiritual. I have high regard for the Stoics of old – like Cato, who walked out into the desert, commanded his servant to bring his sword and fell on it, when he felt his time, usefulness or authority had run out. I think we all want a noble death, and one that gives us the least pain and anguish, but when great men like Nelson Mandela die, we feel like we've lost something more than just a mortal man.

It fell to me to announce the news on 5FM in the early hours of 6 December 2013. I had actually been DJ'ing at a club in Fourways when the station manager called and asked me to come to the studio immediately. I went on air as soon as I arrived and broadcast through the night and into the next morning.

On 23 December 2013, I posted this on my website:

The death of Nelson Mandela has stirred in all of us some powerful emotions and perhaps in some, a desire to retrace the unsteady first steps of a fledgling democracy, even if some of us were too young to experience them first hand.

I am utterly bereft and I never thought I would be. I'm cynical, and I admire cynicism in others; I don't believe in idol worship or iconography; I'm not persuaded by propaganda or politicians, even good ones like Obama. I have been moved and had my heart ripped open by the extraordinary events of the past few days, by the man who manifested them, and by the attention our little country received, punching far above our weight in influence and attention. In a rare failure of the head, the heart won.

Patriotism is a hollow thing, harmlessly put to use in sport, and dangerously wielded by exploitative political forces. National identity and pride are more valuable, omnipresent and useful. Until very recently we didn't have a golden thread to bind us together in this country ... What is it to be South African? I'm not ambitious enough to attempt to answer that, but I can think of a few things we can do to get there:

White people:

1. *South Africa does not belong to you, and it never did. Owning things is a big part of being white: we toil away so that we can own our houses, pay for our children to go to good schools, to buy things that impress other white people. You cannot own a country, and in 1994 nothing was taken away from you that you had any claim to. You need to understand this and show some maturity.*

2. *You are responsible for apartheid, even if you didn't support it, or you were born long after it was dismantled. Your history is the same as the plantation owners of America before the abolition. If African-Americans are still dealing with that inheritance more than 150 years later, you would be callous in the extreme to imagine that black South Africans must somehow 'move on' a mere 20 years since democracy.*

3. *If your guilt keeps you looking inwards instead of out; if you keep building laagers and insist on your culture being under threat from some non-existent foe; and if you keep teaching your children that there was more good than bad before 1990, you are condemning them to irrelevance or exile.*

4. *If the whole wide world is joined in an opinion that is opposite to the opinion you harbour, you're just wrong. And if you're wrong, you can change. If you think they made too much of a fuss over Mandela, or that blacks will never run things as well as whites, or that life in 1983 was better than life is now – you're objectively*

wrong. You cannot allow your own romanticised idea of your youth or a more innocent time to obscure the truth of a brutal reality that went on for other people under your halcyon sky.

5. *Don't tell people, just because you fear change, that things have gone 'far enough' or that you are now the victim of unfair discrimination. You are not. You are still the beneficiary of history, even if you didn't get the job that one time. When you talk about reverse racism or affirmative action you sound like someone who hasn't read enough history books.*

Black people:

1. *I'm sorry. Nothing I can do can rewrite the disgrace of the past. Please believe me that I'm sorry. Not because you have to, but because I care about history, and while I might not have lived through the hopeless, desperate degradations you or your parents did, I have taken the trouble to learn about them. I know you don't trust the white man, and I know they have lied to you for thousands of years, and I don't want you to be my friend – I cannot ask that of you, I only want to be your equal. If you won't accept my apology, we can't get there.*

2. *You have been asked to compromise over and over again. It is not fair, but I will ask that you give even more: taking everything I have will not reverse our roles and give you satisfaction, it will only make you into the same creature that oppressed you. You know how much you hate what racism and apartheid did to your mother, your sister and your own soul. To wish to exact that upon another would mean you have learned nothing.*

3. *Your chief is not your leader and your leader is not a chief. Just as white people have oppressed and asserted an authority they did not have over Africans, a black man who abuses you from a position of power is as much an oppressor. Freedom is something*

you have fought for. Nobody can give you freedom – and once that freedom is yours, they can never take it back, no matter who they are.

4. *Please understand that white people are very easily scared. They're skittish and nervous and other white people once chased the ones that are here in South Africa out of Europe. In the back of their minds, they are waiting for any excuse to run again. They really believe that every black person secretly wants to kill them. Sometimes the dangers they perceive are real (the same dangers you face every day) and sometimes they are irrational and hysterical. Keep telling them everything will be okay. If they feel safe, white people can make a terrific contribution.*

5. *We need to enhance our self-esteem. Black South Africans have been beaten down and told for generations that they're second-rate. You can break that cycle. Yours could be the generation to stand proud in the face of overwhelming odds against you. Nobody can do that but you, and you needn't be lied to or be made to feel inferior again. Don't let racists and sexists and religious bigots of all kinds try to own you or exact loyalty for anything.*

Being black or white is not the most important thing about you. I don't like the collective nouns or classifications people use to describe me. If you want to describe me, use adjectives like funny, ugly, sarcastic or relaxed. Don't say I'm white, rich and young. I'm an individual. Maybe I'm wrong, but I feel that's a healthy attitude. I know black people who behave the way racists think whites should and I know whites who think they're black. They're the most interesting people I know. Don't let us develop a new lexicon for discrimination by calling people chizkops, coconuts or amaqaba.

We have an opportunity to embrace change and take the high road or hide away from each other and turn the fairy tale into a tragedy. I know which I'd prefer ... Do you?

It was against this backdrop, too, that I reflected on my own future in South Africa, opening up to the possibility of a new era. Back in that New York cheesecake shop, our very plain coffee and very rich cheesecake had arrived and a new future was being crafted.

The Finale

On 31 March 2014, when I announced that this was my last show on 5FM, no one saw it coming. There had been rumours – there are rumours every year in the press when contracts are up for renewal – but we had managed to keep this secret a secret. For that first week of April, it was all anyone was talking about. Most people thought it was a bad April Fool's joke, others were curious about what I would be doing and if it was really true that I had resigned.

We had built up an incredible, large and loyal following. Catchphrases we had coined on that show were used in every corner of South Africa. We dominated social media completely, long before any of the other stations and channels had ever even started a Twitter account. It was possibly the most successful morning radio show 5FM had ever had, and only the tiniest handful of people even had the faintest idea that we were about to end it all.

How did I manage to keep it a secret right until the end, you may ask? It was mostly thanks to the disorganisation at 5FM with contract negotiations, and their error in sending me the wrong offer letter. This gave us time to delay our reply. The station manager was herself on the way out and announced her departure a couple of weeks before I announced mine, so her head had already moved on to her new challenge in television. The programme manager blamed the mistake on the Legal Department, who blamed HR, who in turn blamed Legal – just another day at the SABC. A new letter was eventually issued, which gave me more time to plan my new venture.

By the time the second offer letter arrived, it had a seven-day acceptance period. That took us to exactly two weeks before the new contract period was due to start. The timing was so elegant. I wish I could say that I planned it like this, but alas, bureaucratic incompetence was for once my friend. This series of events left the remaining management (who have subsequently left 5FM as well) scrambling. The rest of the 5FM contracts were rolled over for another month and poor Grant Nash was dropped in the deep end and had to 'stand in' for me because the new line-up had not been confirmed. He had to field the overwhelming reaction of disbelief and shock at my departure. DJ Fresh was in Miami and could only move to the now extra-early breakfast show, with a 5 am start, the following month.

The outpouring of support from the public when I left 5FM was a humbling experience. It was only matched later by the support I received when I was axed from the *Idols* judging panel. My radio show is my first love, and being famous is my least favourite part of having a successful broadcasting career, but I had underestimated the power of this special and intimate relationship. These were my extended family and friends; we had woken up together every morning for seven years and had played together every afternoon before that. I couldn't tell them what I had planned for them at that time and I felt guilty for abandoning them. I've never been very good at personal relationships but I live for my radio audience.

In my heart I knew that what I was moving to would serve them better too, in the long run.

Did I Jump or Was I Pushed?

Why did I really leave 5FM? In the increasingly stifling environment of the SABC, as much as I loved my show, and especially my audience, I couldn't have continued working on an annual contract. National elections were coming up and we had been given strict instructions of what we could and couldn't say. I had interviewed Julius Malema when he was still with the ANC Youth League (ANCYL) and wanted to catch up when he left; this had been forbidden. I had enjoyed relative freedom up until then, but the signs of interference were starting to show. When I started CliffCentral.com a month later, Julius was my second guest. Freedom at last.

Each year I contemplated whether it was time to go. Was I still relevant for the station and, quite frankly, was 5FM still relevant for me? Social media had been on the rise and broadcasters were now in the position of growing their own followings on Twitter and Facebook. I had as many Twitter and Facebook followers as I had radio listeners.

The landscape was changing and my audience was increasingly engaging online. 5FM management was talking about starting the breakfast show an hour earlier and that didn't appeal to me at all. Every year they threw out suggestions to see what would stick, and invariably I didn't agree with them. With DJ Fresh hosting afternoon drive and me the breakfast show, the station was at the top of its game and so was I. Was this the time to start messing with a winning formula?

Another thing that irked me was, a couple of months previously, Thabo Modisane's getting suspended for a week for inadvertently not bleeping out the f-word in an audio clip of the Christian Bale rant that went viral. I was furious, not only with management but also with the fact that one complainant – who shouldn't be listening to my show in the first place if they are so sensitive – had been given so much power that the show and the listeners were punished for a week by suspending the executive producer (whom, it so happens, is not prone to swearing himself). In this day and age, is the word 'fuck' still such a big deal? That was another reason to explore new horizons.

During the New York visit I met some interesting people, including Jeremy Coleman, head of programming for Sirius Satellite Radio, who had worked closely with Howard Stern, and our long-time friend and consultant Valerie Geller. We got a glimpse into the new world of netcasting and podcasting. The internet was the only way to go.

Radio is over 100 years old. Guglielmo Marconi is supposed to have patented radio in 1909, and got the Nobel Prize for it. The media at the time, and thus popular opinion, held this to be true. Actually he had stolen the idea from Nikola Tesla. In 1943, the US Supreme Court confirmed – after 34 years – that Tesla, and not Marconi, was responsible for 'conceiving of, and patenting the principles of radio'. Marconi's claim was struck down. Theft is not a great way for any medium to be born, I think you'll agree. Since then, radio's chequered history has run the gamut from being a propaganda vehicle for dictatorial regimes to being a tool for freedom and information in the developing world. Radio engages, connects and entertains millions all over the world. Well, the content does.

Increasingly, technology invented in 1909 seems out of step with things that were invented only ten years ago and exponentially improve almost annually. Mobile technology, the internet and integrated systems all get better faster, and the cost of producing quality content gets cheaper every day. A big media company used to be the only place that could afford to make great content and pay for the licence they needed to broadcast.

Now radio stations have lots of staff, expensive programming, onerous licence conditions, interference from regulators, gerontology of the talent, atrophying of the production processes and a host of parasitic satellite businesses that fight over commission: the above-the-line, below-the-line, digital, social-media, PR, strategic and marketing agencies they need to employ to get their hands on the advertising budgets of large companies. It's perverse. The link between the audience and the product or service is so complicated that viral videos of cats spread with greater ease and less expense. Do you know that Clear Channel, the biggest broadcasting business in the US, with over 850 radio stations, has not made a profit since 2008?

According to publicly released figures, gross advertising revenue for South Africa's broadcasting industry is estimated to have increased in value from just over R2 billion to close to R8.5 billion between 1994 and 2006. It is hard to know just how much is being made now, but, between the major media owners, it's a lot. Much of it is the result of years of brand-building, research, hard work in programming and selling opportunities to advertisers. All that money is made by connecting audiences with products or services. Audiences tune in to hear or see or read things they are interested in, and clients get to sponsor, advertise or outright interrupt that connection in order to get the consumer's attention. Now that the internet is here, a renaissance is so overdue that the baby may well walk out of the womb, fully developed and speaking.

Exactly where I was going, I did not know, but I was absolutely sure that the old ways were not going to work forever. Like the music, movie and publishing businesses, broadcasting has to change. We know that quality content and talent – inspiring, intelligent, entertaining and empowering – will always attract an audience, and we know that audiences change their minds overnight. When the migration to new platforms and the gear shift to new habits takes place, it will do so without warning, and those who don't act fast enough, or who play it safe, will be left with gigantic corporate carcasses and egg on their faces. Just because things have worked one way for a hundred years doesn't mean they always will. If you don't believe me, ask London cabbies what they thought of Uber in 2009, or Kodak what they thought of digital cameras in the 1990s. I'd rather be a Tesla than a Marconi, even if it takes everyone else a while to catch up.

The cliff was high, and there were clouds below, but I had to jump.

The Vision

The big question was always when would be the right time to make the move, rather than waiting to be fired. Professor Jonathan Jansen had once said when I was interviewing him that if you do the same thing for more than seven years, you lack imagination. That stuck with me. Prof Jansen, Vice-Chancellor of the University of the Free State, himself resigned after seven years to take up a post at Stanford University in California in September 2016.

I had been doing the breakfast show on 5FM for seven years. While I give management credit for largely leaving me alone, I felt increasingly stunted. It was time. I needed to be sure what I stood for and what needed to be aligned before I did anything. What did I really care about? I guess this meant I was growing up. Have you ever thought about it – what you really care about?

I came across a saying by Steve Jobs, co-founder of Apple: 'If you are working on something exciting that you really care about, you don't have to be pushed. The vision pulls you.' That statement also resonated with me. What makes you hell-fire, raging mad and what makes you deliriously happy? We should all ask ourselves these things every day.

In order to really call yourself happy, you have to have a brighter future than your present. You need to be invested in tomorrow and not just comfortable with today. When people talk about goals for the year, dream holidays or relationships they want to work on, they're making to-do lists. Vision has to do with the big picture. Vision has to do with how you want people to sum you up when you're finished, when the earth closes over you.

The vision is implemented every day, every year and in every facet of your life – professional, personal, philosophical and intellectual.

How do we get there? Our values are the navigational devices.

There are three things I value: energy, integrity and freedom.

I value energy because it is life: without the nuclear processes that power the stars there cannot be light and heat. Without light and heat there cannot be the fuel and food that sustain us. If you can get out of bed and do something useful and positive, you're spreading the energy of stars back into the universe. You're a part of the wonderful cycle of existence and consciousness. If you just absorb energy, you might as well be a rock or an asteroid. People who emit energy are attractive, alluring and exciting. I value that in all creatures.

Integrity is doing what you say and saying what you mean. It's being honest with yourself, even (and we're all susceptible to a little misstep here and there) when you're not always completely honest with the whole universe. Integrity is a process, an evolution. We fall short of showing true integrity when we're scared, tired, weak, insecure or uncertain. When you're confident, strong, fearless and armed with clarity, you have automatic integrity. Your honesty will make even your bitter enemies begrudgingly accept that there must be verity and value to your words and deeds. Dealing with the obstacles to integrity is part of the experience of living, and allows us to confront our weaknesses and surmount them, not fall victim to their depressing influence.

Freedom is the ability to live according to the maximum extent of your liberty, to exercise independent, unrestricted volition over everything under your control. Freedom does not give you the right to encroach on the freedoms of others. If your freedom expands as far and wide as it is possible to do without limiting the freedom of others, then you're as free as any man or woman has ever been, or will ever be. The exercise of freedom is ongoing and deliberate, even defensive. If it is taken for granted, or left to stagnate, freedom recedes. It is the duty of all living things to patrol the boundaries of their freedom with vigilance. No government, army or god will do that for you. We are objects of nature, species and circumstance and must be responsible for ourselves alone.

When you know what you value, you can start building a vision. Vision takes you beyond the self – an essential part of the comprehensive experience – and allows you to build something of value to others. This may have commercial or philanthropic or systemic application, but without the vision you cannot move to a point of offering anything meaningful to anyone else.

My vision has to be (in a grand and sweeping sense) to leave the world better than I found it. I want to do this in the following ways:

1. To raise the level of discussion from the basic to the material and then from the material to the intellectual. This is something I will strive for, and hopefully succeed in, because, determined as I might be, there will be occasions where my own faculties find themselves limited or insubstantial for the task at hand.

2. To create a free exemplary life for myself that will demonstrate to others that it is possible to live a great life and do great things for those who do not, without irony. I want to live well while exercising my objectives, in luxury and happiness and with as many options as I can exploit at any given time. Mine will not be a life of suffering or deprivation. There is no nobility in poverty. I want to make myself happy so that there is surplus happiness for everyone else.

3. To gather together all the powerful, positive, sincere influence I can muster (in myself and in others) so that I can make statements with authority and get people thinking for themselves. Since I do

not seek to have my hands on the levers of power, I seek to be the voice of reason ringing in the ears of those who do. I want people to know that they can take control of nothing until they take responsibility for themselves. This is not my opinion; this is the next step in our evolution as a species.

4. To build and create physical things that give people hope and engender appreciation of work, responsibility, creativity and honourable activity. These may be places, gatherings, experiences or written articles. Since there can be no altruism, this will satisfy the ego while I am alive, but they will be the things that continue the work when I am gone, because a vision should not die when the principal does.

5. To oppose forces that seek to inhibit freedom, who work with deceit and who wield power cruelly. These forces may be political, social, cultural or religious, but they must be treated with contempt and made to justify themselves in order to establish whether or not they have any quality at all. There can be no more satisfying victory than the victory over wicked people and the destruction of bad ideas.

6. To engage in all of the above and exact only the absolute minimum of suffering to anyone else. I do not believe life is a zero-sum game. The good, the positive and the generous multiply exponentially when there is kindness and openness and respect. I will try every day not to hurt anyone. Practically, this should be the easiest thing to achieve, but only wide-eyed awareness can ensure it.

7. To fill up every day with great memories and experiences, for I don't believe there is a moment to waste and I will have only these two things to take with me to the grave, whether there is a life after this or not.

If I can do all these things, then the miracle of being alive and being alive NOW can amount to more than mere organic existence. That's what I really care about. That's what makes me angry and happy. These are the things that I grapple with every day.

Whatever I do, it has to fit in with this vision. This is what pulled me to the next chapter of my life. This is what inspired the foundation of CliffCentral.com. Entrepreneurship was about to get real.

But before we get to that, I ran into another problem with – you guessed it – free speech.

PART III

My Side-Chick: Television

'My advice would be if you want to pursue a career in the music business, don't.'

SIMON COWELL

Idols

While my radio show was my first love and CliffCentral.com has become my long-term commitment, *Idols* was my side-chick, which straddled both. While the road at 5FM was sometimes rocky, the *Idols* path was carefree and fun despite the fact that every year brought a new controversy over the judges, the votes or the winner. Not in a million years would I have thought that I would be at the centre of the biggest *Idols* controversy ever.

My first season of *Idols* on M-Net was in 2003, the year I joined 5FM, and it became very much part of my life. Although *Idols* has never been my primary job as such, it was my favourite extramural activity. Some people have no idea that I'm that irreverent radio guy. A lot of people in small towns only know me as the blond judge on *Idols*.

When I was approached to be a judge in the second season of *Idols*, I was only 24 years old. Little was known about me then except that I clearly was unafraid to voice my opinion. I was hired apparently because I was outspoken, which would bring a new dynamic to the judging panel. Every year I think that this is probably going to be the last one, but every year is better than the last. Season 11 was the most successful season of *Idols* to date and season 12 is certainly going to top that. The combined viewership on M-Net and Mzansi Magic increased by 29 per cent from season 10, and season 11 generated over 78 million votes.

This year, I've decided it's time – season 12 will be my last season of *Idols*. I enjoy working with the team and watching the successful candidates develop during the season, but, as with 5FM, every year I reassess my position on *Idols* and whether we're still relevant for each other. I have never wanted to overstay my welcome anywhere. Each year as a team, we have navigated the sometimes-sensitive path together and we all played a part in the transformation of the show, especially with the advent of the Mzansi Magic channel, transitioning *Idols* from being a predominantly white show to something more representative of the South African population.

My *Idols* journey has been colourful. I was hired because I was controversial … and I was fired because I was controversial – a paradox highlighted in the High Court judge's ruling in January 2016. For *Idols* 12, I think I must be the only judge in history that has now been placed by a real judge.

Our long and fruitful affair is now over.

The Taste of TV

Looking back, it's been a great ride. The first season of *Idols* was also my first lesson in handling 'fame'. I was young, it went to my head and I thought I was a great big star.

Fortunately that was short-lived. I've seen much more famous people than I will ever be handle fame in better and worse ways: Britney Spears went into meltdown; Justin Bieber allowed himself to be managed, and then became unmanageable as well; Chris Brown started self-destructing; and Leonardo DiCaprio retreated into his work. Some start taking drugs, get into sex scandals, fire their managers or treat their fans badly. I'm glad that I had the wherewithal to see what was happening and start growing up … well, mostly.

When you become part of a stellar show like *Idols*, people start to notice you. Remember, when they asked me to join the panel, I had appeared on TV only once or twice, and I liked the semi-anonymity that radio gives you. By this I mean people might have recognised my voice, but a lot of my listeners hadn't seen my face. Lucky them. I thought I had made it, but I knew nothing.

Remember how I said I'm not comfortable with the way I look? Well, TV made that much, much worse. Suddenly I was getting emails from people who didn't even know that I did a radio show, calling me every kind of thing under the sun because they thought I was being mean. They brought up the crooked teeth (I refused to wear braces in my teens, despite my parents' best efforts), the thin, lanky body, the droopy eyes, the red nose, the awkwardness of my movements.

It was a nightmare for me. You stop hearing all the good things and only hear the attacks. I suppose that's also part of growing up. You realise that you're not really in much of a position to judge others, since, in the qualitative analysis, you usually come up wanting too.

I can't bear to watch early episodes of that show, because I get so embarrassed about the way I tried so hard to impress. I thought I had to be funny, clever, sarcastic and mean. I was doing what I hated everyone in radio doing – performing. And it wasn't me. Randall Abrahams, who had already established himself on the show during season 1, was also my boss at 5FM, and Rina berated me for getting into a 'pissing contest' with him.

The show got what it wanted out of me – controversy, energy, humour – and the ratings were good. In return, I got a whole new audience. Fortunately more people seemed to like me than hated me. It was just that, as usual, the haters were the most vocal. Suddenly people would stop me in shops and at the airport as though they knew me personally. It was also a new and exciting medium to play with. Like most people, I thought TV was the big time. The truth is that TV isn't all it's cracked up to be. I've always said that I don't love it. I love radio.

TV is maddeningly time-consuming. In 2009 I was approached by Bobby Heaney to do a TV talk show. Bobby was not only Nelson Mandela's personal videographer, but also a renowned television, film and stage producer and director with over 30 best director and best production awards to his credit. My own 13-part series on M-Net, *The Gareth Cliff Show*, seemed like a good idea at the time.

I quickly learned that you spend hours producing, perfecting, prerecording, arranging lights, sorting out sound, going through scripts, rehearsing, blocking, timing and planning. And that's before you even start doing the show. By the time I get to the show, I'm bored and exhausted. I'm an instant-gratification kind of guy, or perhaps I just prefer the fact that live radio is electric and unpredictable. You can't edit things when they're live, and when they're over it's too late to fix anything. For three hours every day I produce live content on radio; on TV, you could spend three hours producing one five-minute bit. That's not a great work/reward ratio. I admire people who do daily TV shows. They work hard for their money, and deserve every cent.

Although Bobby was masterful at editing a lively, 45-minute talk show down to the prescribed 22 minutes (to accommodate commercials in a half-hour slot), for me it was like surgically removing the heartbeat. That also included cutting out anything that could be remotely controversial to fit M-Net's prime-time family viewing. It wasn't altogether a waste, though. I learned an inordinate amount from a fine producer and we had some fascinating panellists on the shows.

Idols is different. The crew we work with is like another extended family. I've worked with the same director, Gavin Wratten – another of South Africa's finest – from my first season to the current one, and *Idols* has to be one of the most successful big-budget productions on South African TV. The judges don't rehearse; we're not involved in planning and we arrive just before the cameras start rolling. I just show up and do my thing. The female judges have a harder time because they have to come extra early for hair and make-up. For us guys it's easy; make-up literally means having your cheeks dusted with powder.

With TV comes a loss of anonymity. On radio we can't see each other, and on TV we can't see you, but we sometimes forget that you can see us. While I'm generally outgoing, I tend to be a bit of a loner, and being on TV thrusts you into the 'celebrity' bracket, where you become public property. While I've never identified with being a celebrity, the question of privacy is an interesting one for me. On one hand, my career in radio and TV necessitates being in the limelight and gathering enthusiastic followers, while, on the other hand, it's so important to protect family and intimate details from the prying eyes of the press. The price of fame is compromised privacy. In America, the price is even higher, with many celebrities having to contend with stalkers and the unrelenting paparazzi, who follow them into restaurants, chase them around their children's schools, hide behind bushes while they're on holiday and stake out their homes. In South Africa, we have it easy.

The fact that my path in life happens to be more public than many is still sometimes a bit surreal. At the end of the day, I'm just an ordinary guy who ultimately wants to leave this earth a better place than I found it.

What fame has taught me is that … 'The haters gonna hate …'

The *Idols* Team

Working with the *Idols* team over the seasons has been especially gratifying – there's great chemistry between all of us. Randall is the longest-standing judge, but Unathi Msengana and I go back the longest and she is particularly delightful to work with. Somizi Mhlongo added a new spark when he joined the judging panel in season 11. He has had his own colourful history of controversy.

Both Unathi and Somizi were involved in social media scandals shortly prior to my *Idols* drama. I bet you wondered how the other judges would receive me after all the allegations on social media and in the newspapers once the court documents became public? All of them called me when I was axed from the judging panel, but I'm sure Unathi and Somizi weren't pleased when their 'indiscretions' formed part of M-Net's press statement and subsequent court documents. In the end, the team spirit that we have shared and bonds we have formed over the seasons prevailed.

Randall joined *Idols* in the first season, in 2002. His fellow judges were Sony Music boss Dave Thompson, radio personality Penny Lebyane and PR executive Marcus Brewster. Randall had been the station manager of Good Hope FM in Cape Town in the 1990s before moving to Johannesburg, where he became station manager of the fledgling 'youth' station, YFM. He then moved to SABC to become the general manager of commercial radio in 2002, at the time I moved to 5FM.

Randall is genuinely grumpy but also very funny, and knows more about music than anyone I have ever come across. People think he's serious, dismissive and rude, but he's actually shy. He doesn't like meeting people for the first time. By the 23rd time, he'll warm to you, though. Anele Mdoda, another long-time radio colleague, once told me the story of how she and Randall were at some club in Cape Town. (Interestingly enough, apart from being outspoken, Anele and I went to the same high school, the same university – where we studied the same subjects – and we both started our radio careers at Tuks FM campus radio.)

But I digress ... Anele and Randall were both doing shots of tequila and some girl came up and said hello to them. Anele greeted her and asked her how she was doing, what was new in her career and what the family were up to. Randall just said 'hi' and turned away without as much as a smile. The girl eventually left, obviously a little annoyed at Randall. Anele turned to him and asked, 'You don't know who that is, do you?'. He said no. She reminded him that it was the winner of the previous year's *Idols* show. He had no idea. Now, a lot of people think that's mean and disrespectful, but that's Randall. He's not interested in social niceties and vapid conversation; he's interested in music – *very* interested in music. Randall can tell you every single thing that has ever been written or said about Elvis Presley, the Louvin Brothers or Prince. He saw Prince in concert more times than Bieber has had birthdays. If you sing badly, don't understand the song, mispronounce a word, mistime a phrase or do anything to annoy him, he will hate you.

Unathi and I met when she was a presenter on a TV show called *Castle Loud*. That was when she was known as Unathi Nkayi, before she married fellow DJ Thomas Msengana, better known as Bad Boy T. We were both 23. She was breathtakingly beautiful, and she was always happy. Happy people are worth spending time with and we had a pretty wild introduction. We were at Sun City to see the Irish boy band Westlife. After the concert, we ended up singing with them in the bar until security forced us all to leave in the early hours of the morning. Unathi, it has to be said, sang a bunch of Motown songs and we were all blown away. You have to remember that this was long before she was a professional musician herself, so I suppose you could consider it some kind of initial public performance. Vodka and Red Bulls provided the fuel for our impromptu karaoke session and we ended up getting to know the Westlife guys pretty well. I helped Shane Filan find a diamond ring for the girl he ended up marrying.

I was doing the breakfast show on 702 at the time, and I invited Unathi to be a contestant on my own version of 'Radio Survivor', where I made her, Isobel Jones, Giant the Gladiator, Cyril Green and a bunch of other mismatched celebs compete in off-the-wall challenges, eat disgusting things and sing songs to survive elimination. Unathi narrowly lost out to Isobel and Giant in the finale, but she slayed the singing competition. It should have been obvious that she would become a famous singer a few years later. She already had a show on YFM and we stayed in touch, even if we had shows that were on at the same time, and I was thrilled when she joined *Idols*.

With Unathi Msengana, backstage at Idols, *2015.*

Unathi is a phenomenal mother, wife and professional, and I love her to pieces. We have shared dressing rooms, crude jokes, political and work gossip sessions, and many drinks. It's admirable that she has an abiding love for her Xhosa heritage. Her parents are tremendously successful, modern people too, but she goes back to their farm in the Eastern Cape regularly, dresses in traditional costume and observes all the rituals of her people. That's something you don't necessarily see a pop star, radio DJ or businesswoman do every day.

Somizi is also adept at juggling several careers – actor, singer, dancer and now radio and television personality. He is like a whirlwind. Before he even became a judge on *Idols*, I offered him a show on CliffCentral. com – and he accepted immediately. This was his first break in radio, but he went on to land a prime-time slot on Metro FM. He thinks he can, and he really can, do anything. I remember our first meeting was when he was choreographing the dancers on the 'Spectacular' show and I thought he was off-the-charts crazy. When he joined the judging panel the following year, he brought a much-needed breath of fresh air. You actually can never tell what is going to come out of his mouth, and if he doesn't like you … 'Woo … shem!'

The first time I interviewed Somizi on my show he opened up about his life: his talented parents, Mary Twala and the late Ndaba Mhlongo, who put him on stage as a child; his teenage daughter; his many relationships; his sexuality; his attitude to money; and his love of performing. When you get to interview someone like Somizi, you just shut up and let him talk. Once he feels comfortable, he'll tell the most amazing stories – and he did. He's funny, clever, connected and extraordinarily talented, but I wouldn't last a day in his fast-paced life. I don't know when he sleeps, or how he keeps going like he does – and he's a few years older than me! If you want to know who the 'It-girls' rely on for advice, or if you want to talk to a government minister, Somizi can make it all happen. He also has fabulous nails, a constantly changing hairstyle and a wardrobe that Elton John would give up David Furnish for. When I asked him what it feels like to come from a famous family of actors, singers and dancers, he told me that he's sure his parents would have abandoned him if he hadn't been talented. I believe him.

Complementing the panel is presenter Tebogo 'ProVerb' Thekisho. ProVerb joined *Idols* as co-host with Liezel van der Westhuizen in season 6 and became sole host the following year, as well as becoming co-producer. Just as so many of the M-Net audience might not have known that I was a radio presenter, many wouldn't have known that ProVerb is also a famous rapper. He's also renowned as being one of the few rappers who doesn't swear in his songs. That's Pro, clean-cut and one of the nicest guys I know, but even he didn't manage to escape press scrutiny with his recent divorce – the price one pays for being in the public eye.

Before ProVerb, Somizi and Unathi, my judging colleagues were singer Mara Louw and Dave Thompson, with Colin Moss as the presenter. Some of the most entertaining times on *Idols* were actually when the cameras weren't rolling. Mara was a famous singer in the 1970s and 1980s, and during her time on *Idols* she became infamous for her strange behaviour. For what it's worth, she made me laugh and told me lots of good stories about Miriam Makeba and Manto Tshabalala-Msimang. I liked Mara. Dave, who used to be the head of A&R at Sony Music, was funny too. He had a dry sense of humour, which the cameras didn't pick up.

Colin Moss was our Ryan Seacrest. He was the good-looking one. In fact, Colin was voted South Africa's sexiest man that year, I think. By some strange twist of fate, I also topped the *Heat* 100, which was a great source of amusement to my family and friends, but mostly to me. That same year, *Cosmopolitan* approached me to be in their calendar of sexiest men. I thought it was a joke but Rina said that, since I was 24 at the time, this might be my last chance to be in something like this. I was reluctantly dragged to the photo shoot. I didn't have a six-pack. I did have crooked teeth. I didn't have a golden tan over rippling biceps. How on earth did this skinny, gangly twenty-something end up as Mr August? When the chosen photograph was sent to us for approval, Rina was a bit concerned and mentioned to the editor that there were dark rings under my eyes (not uncommon!). 'Oh, it doesn't matter,' she said, 'Gareth wasn't chosen for his looks.' I rest my case.

Being stylish isn't one of my priorities. The presenter and contestants on *Idols* have clothing sponsorships, but we judges take care of our own wardrobe. I have endless fights with Rina about what to wear for *Idols*. I'd probably just wear shorts and T-shirts if it were up to me. I've never been able to use my appearance to improve my appeal, so I never really gave clothes much thought. The problem is that I also hate being told what to wear. I have refused to use a stylist. Rina is, as usual, absolutely right; the way you dress says something about you. I'm not a slob. I like looking sharp, and when I do wear a suit I think I look okay. Can you imagine how difficult it is to manage me? Rina deserves a giant gold medal.

When you spend as much time doing a show as we have on *Idols*, you

Idols, *the early days with Dave Thompson, Mara Louw and Randall Abrahams.*

develop really tight friendships. Although we judges didn't see much of each other when we weren't recording the show, we'd meet the following year and it would be like old times. Fortunately, many of the artists we discovered have gone on to have personal, financial and career success, and some have even changed the business quite significantly.

While my *Idols* journey is ending, the good memories and friendships will live on.

Behind the Scenes

There are a few questions that people always ask me about *Idols*, so let me try to answer those now. If you're not interested in *Idols*, you can skip the next bit, okay?

Don't you get bored sitting there watching all those auditions?
No. Do you get bored watching them? The fact is, the producers sit through the tens of thousands of auditions and pull out the really good ones and really bad ones to appear before us, and that makes the show interesting. The mediocre people who would bore you and me to death are excluded from the whole process – and a good thing too. We only have to see between 80 and 100 people a day in the audition phase, so it's not too taxing. As for those people who claim it's terribly unfair to cut out some of the average people and leave in some of the terrible ones, I remind you that this is primarily a TV show, not your ticket to stardom. I do sometimes get bored after the auditions, though ... sitting through many middle-of-the-road performances as we sift through the top 16 ... and then I perk up again as we head for the finale.

Is Randall really so mean?
Yes, but it depends entirely on how coddled you were as a child and

what you consider 'mean' to be. If you're talking about being honest with people, then yes, he's awfully mean. If you think he's excessively rude and destructive and cruel, then he's only a little bit mean. Remember, nobody forces those contestants to come to auditions; they come because they want us to tell them whether they have any talent or not. Telling them the truth is a service we provide. Hurting their feelings is, at least some of the time for Randall, a bonus. Randall takes music very seriously, so seriously that it's almost like religious zeal. A bad singer is an insult to a good song. Remember, this is a guy who can tell you everything about Elvis and very little about human emotion. Being upset by him is something you deserve if you thought you'd get something else.

What was Mara Louw like, and what happened with the vodka?
Mara was fun to work with. I said it many times on the show, and I said it in my previous book – she's a nutcase. That doesn't mean I don't like Mara; in fact, I'm very fond of her, but she was a little cranky and inconsistent at times – like Paula Abdul on *American Idol*. *Idols* gave Mara a new lease on life in terms of the entertainment business, but she underestimated how the TV audience would judge her just as she might judge the contestants. It's not like getting up to sing in front of an adoring crowd. Negative feedback eventually washed off of me, but it hurt poor Mara. She was older, and was used to people showing her some deference. Being on TV is hazardous. The vodka incident was one of the more memorable Mara moments. It's not common practice to have a drink on set, but that evening one of the crew brought a bottle of vodka for a pre-show celebratory drink. I passed Mara her drink and all was well until halfway through the show when she became a touch emotional, or maybe delirious. Needless to say, the press had a field day and I was the one Mara threw under the bus during a radio interview the next day. She said that I had given her the vodka, which

had reacted with her medication. Just for the record, I'm not the kind of person who keeps a half-jack handy in case of emergencies, and that incident was about as close to a raucous backstage party as *Idols* ever got. That sort of thing only happens in the movies. M-Net nevertheless took it so seriously, you'd have thought the whole crew would be sent to the Betty Ford clinic for substance abuse ... That was Mara's last season on *Idols*.

What do you know about music?
A lot of people are annoyed that I was made a judge instead of them. I suppose if I got defensive I could go into a whole spiel about how much I know, how long I've been on radio, or that I can sing, or figure out harmonies, or play an instrument, but I don't care about impressing the people who bring this up. You don't have to agree with me; some of the contestants don't listen to anything I say anyway. If you're sitting at home, watching *Idols*, *you* are the judge. By the time we get to the top 16, you actually have a say. I don't. I don't get to choose the winner, *you* do.

Are the judges scripted?
I get a lot of questions about whether or not we're scripted, or whether we're told to put certain people through and others not. First of all, we have never been given a script. Sometimes Gavin Wratten will ask us nicely to say something so he can use it for a promo or something, and we can't even get that right. The poor man has nevertheless weathered the storm well over the course of 12 seasons, and Randall especially drives him crazy by listening to not a single word of instruction. As for Somizi, I dare you to try and script him!

Is it different watching live or on TV?
Yes it is. Sometimes the audience at home has a completely different

experience to us. The live (and loud) crowd is often so enthusiastic that we have to wear headphones to hear the singing. The processing of audio that takes place between the live show and your TV means we sometimes hear a different sound too. Occasionally, when I see the show on TV, I disagree a lot with my own comments. Even we judges disagree with each other, and nobody's ever 100 per cent right – because music isn't science, it's art.

Why are all the winners never heard from after they win?
If you start at the top, there's only one direction you can go in, right? That's true in terms of publicity anyway. The winner of *Idols* is at their zenith in terms of media attention when they win. That interest diminishes with every day that goes by after the finale. That doesn't mean the artist is a failure; it just means that if you're really interested you'll have to go to their gigs, buy their albums or visit their website, like you might if you're an AC/DC fan. I don't see AC/DC on the front page of every paper every day. In fact, I haven't seen them in the papers since the 1980s. They're not failures. I'd give my right nut to watch Angus Young play the guitar, and if I don't hurry up and go to see them play live they might be dead before I get the chance. Don't conflate the amount of attention someone gets with success. Kelly Clarkson was the first American Idol, she's a different story. When last did you hear from Ruben Studdard? The TV show is the star, not the winner.

Those are the most common questions. But *Idols* isn't just about the judges and the contestants. Sitting at home watching the show, *you* are the judge at every step of the journey. You choose a favourite, become distraught when he or she is voted off the show and threaten to never watch again, and then you pick a new favourite. This process repeats itself until only two are left and you back one of them. And you get to judge the judges. Along the way you get some really good entertainment: the laughs, the tears, the songs, the judges' shenanigans, the mishaps and the performances. The show is about you.

Behind the scenes on *Idols* is actually happening in your living room.

Winners' Woes

Being a popular reality show is bound to yield a variety of controversies. This past year has been one where 'White Privilege' became a hot topic, with several racial incidents on social media. The racial controversies on *Idols* began with the very first season, in 2003, when Heinz Winkler was crowned the winner, beating Brandon October, who was a crowd favourite. There was talk at the time that race and privilege contributed to his win. That became a theme over the next few years, but in those days it wasn't magnified by social media to the extent it is today.

Remember season 2, when Anke Pietrangeli beat Poseletso Sejosingoe? Progress was made in season 3 when Karin Kortje and Gift Gwe were the finalists, with Karin edging Gift out to be crowned the winner. It was a heart-warming story for the humble apple-picker from Grabouw, who transformed into a diva after her win until … well … until her boyfriend was arrested and subsequently convicted for the murder of a Durbanville guesthouse owner. Since that scandal, we haven't heard much about Karin.

Season 4 saw another young coloured winner from Cape Town, Jodi Williams, and then another one in season 5 … well, almost. Sasha-Lee Davids of Cape Town was announced the winner, which was received with boos from runner-up Jason Hartman's supporters. It turned into a huge controversy, with M-Net issuing a statement the next day announcing Jason Hartman as the real winner owing to a voting count glitch – if you can call 200 000 votes not counted a *glitch*.

So that year we had two winners. Elvis Blue and then Dave van Vuuren won the next couple of seasons before *Idols* was screened on M-Net and Mzansi Magic, and for the first time there was a black winner – Khaya Mthethwa. After that we had Musa Sukwene the next year, then Vincent Bones and, in 2015, Karabo Mogane. Season 12 is being screened only on Mzansi Magic, so the transformation is now complete. Dare I say it's time for a woman to win?

When white people tell me the show is too black, I remind them what black people used to tell me in season 2 – that it was too white. I'm really proud of the way we judges, the producers and M-Net adapted and moulded the show into the biggest representative reality TV show in South African history.

While the *Idols* digital presence has also increased over the last few years, in the earlier years – long before we had hashtags and handles – my own social media platforms became a primary forum for *Idols* fans and haters. I pioneered the first online discussions, which went on after the TV shows ended, and opened up conversations on Facebook that got people talking about race, talent and music. It was sometimes very hairy. There were a lot of nasty things said right at the beginning, and there are still nasty things being said. That's human nature.

During one season a few years back, when *Idols* was still only on M-Net and regarded as a 'white' show, I made a comment that I thought we would have a black winner that year. It was the year that Elvis Blue won over Lloyd Cele – I was sure Lloyd was going to win that year. This comment raised the hackles of some coloured people, who felt I was dismissing the success of all the winners from those communities. I also found myself in the newspapers again in another race row, being called a racist – this time by a few white people. Many of them, so patently obsessed with the race of the contestants themselves, expected me to be dishonest enough to pretend that race was not one of the single biggest factors in any sphere of South African society. I'm afraid I couldn't do that.

These same people insisted that they saw race as a non-issue, but proceeded to post the most scathing and derogatory things on various social media platforms that evidenced their inability to see talent in all its multicultural, diverse glory. It hardly mattered that a few weeks later some black people were calling me a racist, this time over my 'Dear Government' letter. Do you suppose the two badges cancel each other out?

Even then, I addressed the race issues on my radio show and in my blogs. I noted that, with the growth of social media, people who join the public conversations seem to be more comfortable saying things online that they wouldn't say face to face. A degree of anonymity allows for civility to be suspended, while deep-seated anger and insecurities ooze out like when a boil is lanced. I often wondered if this was the forum that might genuinely allow the poison to surface and, in time, facilitate our coming to a place of more openness, to bring to our vibrant multicultural society an acceptance of the richness of our diversity. I don't know whether it will. It seems to have got much worse with the passing years.

Events took an unexpected turn in January 2016. In the light of these events, and my own *Idols* controversy, in which comments on Twitter were presented in court by M-Net as grounds to get rid of me, I find all of this just a little more than slightly ironic. Twitter was now the judge, jury and research panel.

Even to the untrained eye, this seemed to be a curious strategy to guide corporate decision-making.

The Longest Month of My Life

It all started as the New Year started. CliffCentral had settled down nicely and we happily celebrated our second Christmas and New Year since launching on 1 May 2014. The entrepreneurial journey is not for the faint-hearted, but we ended the year on a high note, with sponsorship starting to pick up nicely. Nevertheless, I began the year with a feeling of trepidation. While I was wading through the Sunday night blues and trying mentally to prepare myself for the first show of the year, I had no idea that I was about to embark on the longest month of my life.

I knew I wasn't ready to be back at work. After many years of hosting a breakfast show, this was the first time I wished I had taken another week off. That in itself was a bad sign, but worse was to come. I love doing my morning show; it's the most exciting way for anyone to start the day. You get all the news first, you get to help everyone else digest whatever is going on, and you get to work before the traffic. Actually, that's the best reason right there. I hate traffic that much.

January is meant to be the month of new beginnings – back to school, back to work, New Year's resolutions. Everyone is full of vim and vigour. I wasn't feeling it. With what followed, maybe the rest of South Africa wasn't either. There had been a strange malaise in the nation since the President, famous for blunders both great and small, had made possibly his most devastating cock-up to date: He fired a perfectly competent Finance minister, Nhlanhla Nene, and appointed a complete nobody. You know what happened afterwards – the rand spiralled down the drain and the stock market was stripped of hundreds of billions of rands. Thankfully, sanity prevailed and he corrected his error, but we have never fully recovered. I think many of us went back to work in January filled with dread.

But that was just a teaser for what was to come. Following the New Year's celebrations, a little-known and obviously ignorant KwaZulu-Natal coastal estate agent called Penny Sparrow wrote an odious social media post about crowds of black people on the beaches – comparing them to monkeys. Now, in the real world, people would rightly dismiss

Penny Sparrow as a nutty old bigot and move right along, but on social media a massive storm was brewing.

On Monday morning I dealt with this on my show on CliffCentral. com, and unequivocally condemned her racism. We all did. I don't remember anyone sensible saying anything even nearly like 'You know, I kinda think she has a point …' But, as we have all learned, Twitter is also a maelstrom of malcontents, a dominion for the disenchanted, and a new home for the trolls that used to spread their vitriol on News24's now-defunct comments section.

It turned out that Penny Sparrow was also a member of the Democratic Alliance (DA). The DA leader, Mmusi Maimane, in a clear attempt to showcase how authentically black the new DA was (and how the party empathised with the mass of justifiably angry black people), issued a statement about how some forms of speech should be criminalised. The fact is that whenever there is pain, anger or sorrow, politicians arrive on the scene and capitalise on the situation to build their own support. We should see through it, but we often don't. Many people thought that the Penny Sparrow saga was a coordinated ANC initiative to serve as a distraction from the President's foibles.

In response to Mmusi's comment, someone drew up one of those snap polls on Twitter, asking people for their opinions on criminalising hate speech. I retweeted it and commented with that now infamous tweet:

Gareth Cliff ✓
@GarethCliff

People really don't understand free speech at all:

Having already discussed the whole Sparrow saga on my show, I wrongly assumed that we were all already in agreement about Penny Sparrow and this blatant racism being something totally abhorrent.

My ill-timed tweet became the source of unrelenting anger, name-calling and death threats against me as the message vanished in the shitstorm. A handful of angry people responded to my tweet to say I was defending Penny Sparrow. Others responded to those tweets, and then more responded to those tweets, and so it spiralled into what I called #SparrowGate, causing disproportionate outrage on social media. By the way, I've noticed that, as a rule on social media, a person's level of anger is often inversely proportional to the number of followers they have. In other words, you'll find that someone shouting in an empty room usually says the vilest things of all. I call it Arsehole's Law.

Rina instantly saw that this was a problem. I couldn't, but as the pack of hungry online wolves fixed their gaze on me, I became, for the first time, very worried. Normally I had reasoned or charmed my way out of situations like this, but this time it was different. It felt like the searchlights were on me, that I was the designated prey, and that all those revolting things Sparrow had said were being attributed to me. It was as if the hunt would bag a much more satisfactory quarry if it were I who fell, rather than some obscure woman in southern KwaZulu-Natal.

Something sinister was brewing.

#SparrowGate

Whether this was a coordinated plot or not, we will never know for sure, but the lynch mob was suddenly at my digital door. There were calls to boycott me, and even *Idols*, as the mob directed their full fury at me. Considering my own Twitter following was 1.2 million at the time, it was only a handful of tweeters who were warring, but they were loud. While Rina despaired about my poor timing, knowing it would be misconstrued, she also quickly identified what she called 'The Dirty Dozen' – the main instigators in this Twitter onslaught. Familiar names from previous attacks kept popping up in a pattern that suggested a more coordinated approach.

After the first 24 hours of abuse and accusations, I lay down on the sofa in our office the next morning. I was miserable. I have often said that for most of my life I haven't understood (in any real, personal sense) what it means to be depressed. That feeling that you'd prefer the ground to swallow you up rather than face the day, the void without answers … I had never been there before. My default factory setting seems to be 'happy'. I never hold grudges or stay angry or sad for very long. That morning I was unable to see the light at the end of the tunnel. I questioned all the things I had always thought to be true. I felt like running away, I couldn't do anything. I just lay there.

We had just started a new business, CliffCentral.com, and it wasn't even two years old. Anyone who starts something new like that knows it's tough as nails. In the economy of South Africa, in 2016, that was going to be even harder. We had a wonderful, talented, small staff complement – people I was suddenly responsible to and for. Before Rina or I could pay ourselves, we had to make sure they all got paid. If this business failed, many years of brand-building, experience, value and risk would go up in smoke and people would lose jobs. Suddenly I found myself staring down the barrel of that scale of failure. I felt viscerally sick.

While I was lying there, trying to contemplate how all of this happened, Tumi Morake came into the office. She was about to start a brand-new show with my on-air partner, Mabale Moloi. Both of them could tell I wasn't in a good place. I decided to ask them what they thought I should do; perhaps there was an answer they could glimpse through the fog. Mabale had worked with me for almost ten years, and we had weathered a few storms together. I hoped she'd have an idea.

Both Tumi and Mabale thought I should apologise, not to those people who had never liked me and thought I was a racist, but to those who had listened to me for years on radio and followed me on social media, who supported me but might not have even seen the tweet and thought they might be 'losing' me. They did agree that the timing of my tweet was insensitive and could lead to being misinterpreted. That's what needed to be clarified. I decided to take their advice: and posted my next tweet, which sadly only led to more vitriol.

Here is the apology:

Gareth Cliff @GarethCliff   2h

I've been an insensitive asshole many times. This whole saga with the idiotic comments of Penny Swallow has upset me, but I must acknowledge the pain and anger of so many on Twitter who thought I would in any way condone the things she said. If you thought I was on the side of a racist,

I assumed we were all already in agreement about how you can't stand up FOR racism. If I didn't make that clear, I apologise - sincerely.

With regard to free speech and hate speech, I need to continue my education.

G

Muzi Kuzwayo and Phumi Mashigo, two old friends, popped in the next day while I was sitting in the office, vacant and miserable. Muzi has been a success in advertising and many other creative pursuits for a long time and is someone whose opinion I value. Both he and Phumi, who hosts a show on CliffCentral.com, did their best to lift my spirits. Muzi, along with several others who understood the intention of the tweet, wondered why I had apologised. 'Fuck them!' he said. That made me smile, the only smile I had cracked that week. A week later he brought me one of his most treasured possessions – a magnificent book of photographs of Muhammad Ali, including quotes, interviews and stories about the champion and his life. Muzi pointed out several situations where the great Ali could have given up and given in, but didn't, and he urged me to remember him as I took on the fight ahead. Sadly, we lost Ali in June 2016 after his long struggle with illness.

DJ Sbu, along with other colleagues, including Ferial Haffajee, Justice Malala, Monwabisi Thethe and Tumisho Masha, risked insult themselves and supported me publicly. The difference was that these were people who actually knew me personally and not strangers being swept up by the Twitter frenzy. DJ Sbu, also no stranger to controversy, was a guest on my show during that week and posted a video of the show on Instagram and Twitter, saying:

> I think the people calling Gareth racist should first look around @ CliffCentral.com studios & see how many intelligent talented black people he has empowered. I have known this man for many years. He usually tells it like it is & pisses off a lot of people but I can bet my last Mofaya CAN he's the last person to be racist. Keep your head up @GarethCliff getting fired is nothing new to entrepreneurs. Its time to move from good to GREAT! All the best for the new year.

Many other high-profile people supported me privately, and literally thousands of encouraging comments online fuelled the fight in me during those moments when I was ready to throw in the towel. It allowed me to keep things in perspective and not to lose sight of why I had started CliffCentral.com in the first place. I will always be grateful to the people who expressed their support, especially those colleagues who found themselves in the firing line.

It was important for me not to lose the vision. As a white guy, I'm mindful that I inherit a system biased in my favour, but I'm also a passionate South African and have been outspoken about issues since I was at school. I posted a blog on my website and Facebook at the time and urged that 'we should not be deterred from continuing the discussions we need to have to build a better South Africa – to continue to engage constructively – tell our stories, share our ideas and LISTEN to each other; we should not be bullied and that we should not tolerate racism'. Judging by the positive comments on Facebook, it seemed the vitriol was confined to Twitter.

We understand the world through the complex filters of our genetic inheritance and our circumstances – nature and nurture. I can't do anything about the circumstances of my inheritance or the kind of childhood and opportunity life bestowed on me, any more than can someone born of sexual assault to a single mother in poverty. It is what it is. The character of a person, however, can be determined based on how they respond to what life throws at them – good and bad.

You can't assume someone will fit into any of the boxes we like to conveniently categorise them into, and you have to actively work against our instinctive mammalian pattern-seeking impulse in order to appreciate the individual. If we can't defeat this impulse, we can't evolve and we can't defeat racism and prejudice. The most evil thing about racism, anti-Semitism, homophobia or any other kind of bigotry is that they allow us to dehumanise and label whole groups of people and, as a corollary, to do abominable, unconscionable things. It has taken me almost 40 years to realise that secular humanism is the only way we can come to grips with and defeat bigotry.

We shouldn't assume everyone is on the same page as us, as I did with Penny Sparrow. It's best to take everything back to first principles. In a world with multiple platforms of expression, there is still a very big chance of being misunderstood. We shouldn't get so wrapped up in our own point of view that we forget that some people may not have the same understanding of the context of that point of view. Sometimes you can control that perception with what you do or don't say.

Sometimes it doesn't matter what you do; some people have already decided and you're screwed.

#IdolsGate

Back to January 2016 and Day 3 of #SparrowGate. The dust was starting to settle. A post on my website and Facebook received over 1.5 million views, with thousands of positive comments, as we gained an understanding of what had transpired. Nevertheless, M-Net put out a statement that they were reviewing my contract as a member of the judging panel on *Idols*. I was called for comment by News24 (I've often been misquoted, but this time they quoted me verbatim):

> Anyone who has been listening to me for the past two decades would pretty much know where I stand and I do not have any support for Penny Sparrow. It irritates me that I have been conflated into an argument with a whole bunch of other people that I didn't start and I wasn't joining the wrong side of. I've worked with M-Net for over ten years and suddenly people are calling on them to boycott me, as if I have been hiding some kind of latent, nasty personality for all of these shows. *Idols* is a talent show about brilliant people in South Africa who deserve a stage and platform for their talent. The fact that a bunch of lunatics on Twitter are starting to make this about them! How dare they? I think my timing was off. The important thing here is that I did not say anything racist and I was not supporting anyone racist.

On day 4, I was asked to go to a private meeting the next day at the M-Net offices. On day 5, together with Rina Broomberg, I met with the CEO, Yolisa Phahle, the head of local interest channels, Nkateko Mabaso, and the head of public relations, Lani Lombard. I was anticipating a discussion as to how we could turn this into something positive, but before we even started we had an inkling of the outcome, judging by everyone's behaviour. We had bumped into the executive producer in reception and she was extra-stressed. With Lani holding back the tears from the onset of the meeting and Nkateko uncomfortably shifting in his chair, it was clear the decision had already been made. I actually felt sorry for Lani. She's been with M-Net for a long time, and we've even negotiated some of the other controversies together. I know she probably tried to come to my defence, but the decision had clearly been made higher up, quite possibly by someone who wasn't brave enough to be in the room.

There wasn't anything to discuss. Rina asked if they had read my blog post that had received such a positive response, or if they had listened to any of my shows that week, especially the one that morning with Advocate Dali Mpofu and DJ Fresh. They hadn't. They wrung their hands and offered the opportunity to do a joint statement. We declined. Rina, who has been in business a lot longer than I, just said: 'You need to do what you need to do and we'll do what we need to do.' At that stage I had no idea what we needed to do. I was partly relieved because I had seriously considered not continuing with *Idols* for season 12, and was partly concerned about how this move would be interpreted, and how it might impact on our little start-up.

Upon leaving the meeting, I turned to them and said: 'If the worst thing you can say about me is that I was on the right side of freedom of speech, then you will find yourself on the wrong side of history.' With that said, I walked out.

Understandably, the demands of angry tweeters to have me removed, as well as the threats of some Mzansi subscribers to boycott, was too scary for M-Net, especially with filming due to start in less than a month. In my experience, it usually takes around seven days for these fires to burn out, so the announcement managed to catch the tail end of this one.

#SparrowGate very quickly escalated into #IdolsGate after M-Net made an announcement (online and on Twitter) in the early hours of Saturday morning that I would no longer be part of the judging panel:

> M-Net today announced that Gareth Cliff will not be part of the judging panel for *Idols* SA Season 12, which is due to commence with countrywide auditions at the end of January 2016.
>
> M-Net thanks Cliff for the critical role he has played in seeking out and developing new talent over the years and for contributing to the success of the show to date.
>
> *Idols* SA Season 12 will be screened on M-Net's Local Interest channel Mzansi Magic which is available to both DStv Premium and DStv Compact viewers.

The M-Net PR machine was up at midnight crafting their announcement while most of us were sleeping. I woke up on Saturday morning to calls from various newspapers for comment. Needless to say, I had no comment at the time, but social media was abuzz again, accusing M-Net of double standards (having axed me but not my fellow judges for their earlier controversial tweets). By this time the initial anger towards me, as anticipated, was dying down and the sentiment was turning.

M-Net reacted hastily to defend the double-standards accusations and posted another statement on Saturday morning:

> Over the last few months following Unathi's indiscretions on so-cial media, we have been in discussions with our judges, presenters

and talent to sensitise them to the risks of using social media. All the *Idols* SA judges were reminded that M-Net holds all brand ambassadors and employees to the highest standards in our ongoing efforts to promote and build a modern and inclusive South Africa.

Unfortunately we then had to deal with Somizi's inappropriate comments and following the latest issue, we have now implemented a zero tolerance policy for all social media posts that go against the spirit of nation-building. This policy will apply to everyone associated with our brands going forward.

We do not believe that Gareth is a racist but his response showed a lack of empathy for our history and it is important to differentiate between freedom of speech and hate speech. Penny Sparrow's comments were hateful. Hate speech is not applicable with regard to freedom of speech.

The stage was set. I had supported both Unathi and Somizi when they had had their Twitter troubles, and I was sorry they had to be dragged in now. Instead of engagement and reviewing the context, M-Net had moved swiftly to try to make an example of me.

Again, had M-Net forgotten what a long road we had travelled together? I hadn't.

Political Pressure?

Many people thought that this was a publicity stunt on M-Net's part. Others speculated that they were bowing to political pressure from the ruling party. My core detractors were mainly ANC cadres, with the ANC Youth League (ANCYL) tweeting a call to march on DStv to have me removed from *Idols*.

The ANCYL had already staged a march to Standard Bank to have economist Chris Hart fired. He was in trouble for tweeting 'More than 25 years after apartheid ended the victims are increasing along with a sense of entitlement and hatred towards minorities.' The racist vitriol these words unlocked was unfathomable, and the poor man also lost his job. Anyway, the reconstituted remnants of the ANCYL decided to march on the Standard Bank headquarters; they managed to muster 20 people or less, and ended up demonstrating outside the wrong bank. If M-Net was worried about these guys, I'm pretty sure they were being paranoid. I doubt those 20 people could spell M-Net.

Minister Razzmatazz, Fikile Mbalula, not only joined the fray on Twitter, again, but was also a guest that week on *Real Goboza* on SABC1. I didn't watch the show, so I'm not sure what he said, but these were just some of the tweets flying around afterwards:

@MissMadiba: That awkward moment when Fikile Mbalula says he's got Gareth Cliff handled & that time he's fired! LOL #RGB

@NakediGreen: Fikile Mbalula: Nah nah don't tell me about Gareth Cliff, I can handle that boy, I'm ready for him. #RGB #jawdrop

@Bosslady_Sne: Fikile Mbalula on RGB says he is ready for Gareth Cliff … haibo I can't wait lo

Really, Mr Minister? The Minister's sidekick, Esethu Hasane, was right behind him with a slew of attacking tweets. It so happens that even he needed freedom of expression explained to him – so my free speech tweet may make sense to him now. While he was tweeting about me during #IdolsGate, Esethu also laid a complaint with the BCCSA against Redi Tlhabi on 702 Talk Radio. Redi commented on her show: 'The dumber people in leadership in government are, the better.' This was a response to President Zuma's statement that 'people should not pay attention to people who talk too much on television because they are educated black people who think they are clever'. Esethu claimed that 'as a university graduate in the employ of government', Redi's comment was 'condescending and degrading' to his dignity.

The case went to the BCCSA, and was eventually dismissed. In the lengthy judgment by the current BCCSA chairperson, Judge Ratha Mokgoatlheng, the crux of my point was stated exactly:

> [16] Inasmuch as Mr Hasane has a constitutional right to freedom of expression, so too does Redi Tlhabi enjoy the same right. The right to freedom of expression is not dependent on the dissemination of acceptable or rational ideas only; indeed, it extends to opinion or views that might be anathema to those who occupy influential positions in society or in institutions.

The Social Justice Warriors glossed over this one, but in our racially sensitive society, however, if I had made this statement it might have become another monumental race row in the Twitter Tribunal. Who knows?

Maybe you can't blame M-Net for buckling under the pressure. Was DJ Fresh right when he tweeted:

What next indeed? It was disappointing that there was no engagement from M-Net, which, I believe, was a lost opportunity to take the high ground and together confront the issues and engage the matter to reach a better understanding. There's a leadership vacuum in this country and it's time we started standing up for, and working towards, unity rather than division. In virtually every season of *Idols* we have dealt with racial issues, and we've always managed to steer our way through it constructively – together.

Being axed because of a 'lack of empathy for the country'? Are you kidding me?

Enter Dali Mpofu

When the proverbial shit hit the fan that first week of January, after I had posted my apology, Advocate Dali Mpofu tweeted:

Dali Mpofu
@AdvDali_Mpofu

Way to go Gareth!I KNOW you are NOT a racist.Now about those FREE lessons on Hate Speech,son...

Dali Mpofu, a prominent advocate and national chairperson of the Economic Freedom Fighters (EFF), had been the big boss when I was at 5FM – he was the CEO of the SABC in 2009. Dali's journey at the SABC was short but colourful, to say the least. He took the SABC to court after he was suspended for suspending the then head of news and current affairs, Snuki Zikalala. Apparently he had accused Zikalala of leaking confidential documents to other media outlets but the board disagreed, saying he had no authority to suspend Zikalala. After a highly publicised court battle, a settlement of around R14 million was negotiated and Dali agreed to withdraw all pending legal actions against the corporation.

I reconnected with Dali Mpofu a couple of years later when I invited him to be a guest on my TV talk show on M-Net. He's an impressive man with a larger-than-life presence and a hearty laugh that lifts the mood in the darkest of moments. It had been my turn to be in the news with the letter I wrote to the government in 2010, and he joked that if ever I were fired by the SABC, he would represent me. Life has strange and mysterious ways of working. Who could have guessed that this would become a reality – only that it would be another corporation and it would happen for one of the most uncontroversial things I've ever been in trouble for – tweeting *People don't understand free speech at all.*

When Dali tweeted, I immediately took him up on the offer and invited him to be on my show on CliffCentral, which he agreed to do that Friday. DJ Fresh was also booked that Friday. Because DJ Fresh and I are on air at the same time, we got him as our guest on the last day of his holiday; fortunately, Dali was still on holiday too, so it would be a happy reunion with Dali Mpofu and DJ Fresh on the show together.

This show broke all records for the most downloaded podcast on CliffCentral. We spoke about the past and the reasons people feel as strongly as they do about hurtful and hateful things. After an hour and a half, we all felt that the tone had been pretty inspiring. We explored the meaning of free speech and the blurred line when it comes to hate speech. It would have been both informative and healing for anyone who may have listened.

After the show, I mentioned to Dali that I had been called to a meeting at M-Net and, judging by their press statement two days before, there was a good chance they would fire me. He said that would be a bad move and that we should let him know the outcome. I did call him after the meeting, but at that stage we didn't know when M-Net would announce it.

Getting litigious is not my way. I don't have a lawyer. Berkowitz, Smirkowitz and Malpractowitz had been our fictitious legal team at 5FM, and now I wished they were real. Everything that had happened in the preceding week seemed a bit unreal, like a bad dream that I was bound to wake up from. More than anything, I just felt numb. This couldn't be happening. I vacillated between asking myself how I could have allowed myself to be so misunderstood and being angry about the country.

I was ready to walk away and let the dust settle. The press was on fire the whole weekend, and Rina fielded it all. She offered no comment but did say that we would get a legal opinion. That caused another wave of reports that 'Gareth Cliff is to take legal action'. At that stage, I honestly didn't know what I would do. The most encouraging part was the avalanche of support I received, not only on social media but also by email and from callers to CliffCentral. I wrote a fairly philosophical blog post that again received over a million views on Facebook. It reminded me why I do what I do – for the listeners who have become my extended family over the years.

Seeing the social media buzz over the weekend, Dali Mpofu called me on Monday. We arranged to meet the next day to talk it through, and he took on the role of a wise counsellor, who had already reached out in the most constructive way.

There are many people who might criticise Dali Mpofu for his position on certain issues, his personal life, even his career in law, but I doubt you'll find one who will tell you that he didn't espouse the cause of the murdered miners of Marikana and their families sincerely and most doggedly. Dali sought justice for these poor people in the face of overwhelming odds and a great deal of political pressure. Public opinion against the government on the way that the massacre was handled was overwhelming – and the subsequent hearings were painful and fractious. Analysts like Justice Malala have said repeatedly that Marikana was the turning point for the ANC and the government, and the beginning of a decline in trust, loyalty and moral rectitude.

Dali felt it was imperative to challenge M-Net's decision to axe me without following due process, and especially given their second statement defending why I had been fired and not the other judges. He said that if I walked away, I would always be remembered as that white guy who was fired for racism. Their decision to axe me would add fuel to the fire for those labelling me racist. That is exactly what happened, with the usual suspects dragging up all the previous controversies they could find in my career as proof that I'm racist.

Rina and I met Dali at his chambers in Sandton. Most people have an office. I have a studio. Advocates have chambers. Dali has a keen mind and a schedule that would terrify some of the busiest people I know, but his chambers look like there might be old, dead clients buried under the mass of law journals, bits of paper, files and furniture.

In Dali Mpofu's chambers with Eric Mabuza (at left) and Rina Broomberg, January 2016.

Don't get me wrong, they're beautifully appointed and full of necessary and interesting things, but it's an explosion of papers and files. Although he knows where everything is and works away furiously at whatever open surface he can find, it would take every servant on *Downton Abbey* a week to start sorting the place out.

Dali suggested I ask for reinstatement as well as compensation for defamation, but that wasn't on my mind at the time. He asked if I had a lawyer; I didn't. He recommended Eric Mabuza, and while I didn't know him, any recommendation from Dali Mpofu was good enough for me. Those who cynically claimed that it was a deliberate strategy on my part to hire a black lawyer to prove something were wrong. While many government departments and black-owned businesses don't make adequate use of black legal professionals, I was pleased to trust my entire reputation to these two men. Eric Mabuza was the best person to represent me.

We met Eric for the first time two days later. While we waited in reception, many people walked by and stared knowingly; one even pointed – that's the guy who was just fired from *Idols*. Some people felt uncomfortable when they saw me, like when someone has died and you don't know what to say.

Rina caught sight of Eric before I did. She was facing the door and said something like: 'John Legend is about to walk in.' I thought she had lost it, that the stress of the whole situation had suddenly flipped a switch in her head. With that, Eric Mabuza walked over and shook our hands as though we had known each other for a long time. He did look like John Legend, and he had the same cool, calm and collected demeanour. I imagine that most people approach a lawyer only when things are going horribly wrong in their lives, and it makes a big difference if that lawyer is stoic, confident and soft-spoken. It's almost like they're saying, 'I've got this, and there's nothing to worry about.'

Later on, when I saw his car number plates I asked him if he was from Limpopo, and it turns out he was. Eric is all about the business, but I did learn that he grew up in a township outside Tzaneen in Limpopo province and obtained his first degree at the University of Limpopo. He later went to Wits to finish his honours degree and did his articles at the law firm of Edward Nathan & Friedland. So you see, Limpopo does have talent!

Dali was having lunch at a restaurant across the road and we joined him. After a fairly brief and surprisingly leisurely lunch, it all seemed very straightforward. Eric insisted that we had to go for reinstatement as a matter of urgency since *Idols* was due to start filming in three weeks. Defamation was also a certainty since Dali thought we needed to restore my reputation, damage to which he believed M-Net had reinforced, if not instigated. With that, I left things to my legal team. It took minutes for the first tweet to be fired off that 'Somewhere in Sandton, @DaliMpofu is handing @GarethCliff an EFF membership card'.

There is a terrific relief in handing the things you can't control or understand to people who can. Eric, as unassuming as he is, is a man of action. Once I had emailed him everything he needed – the tweets, the M-Net statements, the emails with regard to arrangements for season 12 and my last few contracts – he got going. That was the first night I had a fairly good night's sleep in over a week.

The next morning, Eric arrived at CliffCentral with a letter to be served to M-Net that I had to sign. I hardly had time to take it in but it was the first time I realised the magnitude of the whole situation: R25 million or reinstatement! Another headline was about to flash across all the newspapers: 'Gareth Cliff Sues M-Net for R25 Million'.

House of Cards

The letter to M-Net was summarily delivered to the M-Net CEO and to Sic Entertainment (the production company) because the contract was between both those parties and me. I felt bad that the production company had to be dragged into the matter, because I've worked with them since my first season of *Idols*. Gavin Wratten and Anneke de Ridder are consistently committed and hard-working people, people I consider friends. Over 11 seasons, they had become another satellite family to me, and we had laughed, cried, travelled and philosophised together. I was pretty sure that they didn't want me fired.

Rina emailed Anneke; since all her other emails to Anneke to confirm season 12 are now very much in the public domain and the main exhibits in court to debate the existence of a contract, here was the follow-up, which you won't have seen yet:

15th January 2016

Dear Anneke

It was good to see you on Friday, albeit under the circumstances. Needless to say that Gareth needs to do what is necessary to protect his reputation – this is all so unfortunate – but we just wanted to thank you and the team for an amazing journey. Even though I personally haven't seen much of you, both Gareth and I have huge respect for Gavin, you and the team and have been very proud to be part of this production.

Wishing you all good things.
Rina

To which Anneke replied:

15th January 2016

Dear Rina

Thanks for your kind words.

This past week has been one of the more difficult ones for me not only on a professional level, but also on a personal level. I have been through this thing in my mind soooo many times. Trying to make sense, understand, justify.

It literally feels as if I had lost a family member. And it is not about me, but sitting here and reading your mail – I am crying again.

I have been wanting to talk to Gareth, but I have not had the courage.

I will mail him and maybe come and say hi at CliffCentral next week. Take care and hope to see you soon.

A

Xxx

I think you can tell that there was no animosity there. That is why I felt particularly bad that the production company had to be a co-respondent, but also why it was easy for me to return to *Idols* after the court judgment. There were actually no hard feelings there at all. All three of the other *Idols* judges had also made contact with me, and, despite their being dragged into court documents, our mutual respect and friendship would endure this controversy too. I certainly hoped so, and I was right.

It had all happened so fast that I hadn't had the chance to digest the contents of the letter to M-Net. I admit it made me uncomfortable. I had decided to do what very few freelancers in the South African media industry have dared to do – fight back. You have to understand that, as a freelancer, you're totally disposable, no matter how important you might think you are to this show or that programme. The broadcasters can fire you on a whim, and they see you as totally replaceable. You could even come up with the original idea, find a sponsor, get the show commissioned and do all the work, and they can still take it all away from you and put someone else in your place. They have all the power. That's why so few people stay in television for long, and if they do, you can pretty much guarantee they accepted whatever was thrown at them, and usually very little money, in order to hold on to the job.

M-Net belongs to a much bigger media empire, that of MultiChoice, who in turn belongs to Naspers, the seventh biggest media business in the world, and the most valuable company on the Johannesburg Stock Exchange. One share in Naspers costs more than R2 000. They're a tremendously successful, powerful corporation and they have considerable resources at their disposal.

Never before had they been faced with one of their freelancers on one of their biggest shows taking them on so publicly. I think that, right up to the very end, they were convinced that I would cut and run. I thought about it so many times. The might of their money and their expensive legal representation, not to mention their arsenal of media assets that could be deployed to annihilate me, gave me the chills. I was just a little guy who was trying to get my new media business off the ground. If ever there were a corporate David v Goliath, this was it.

Most of my university friends, now experienced in the legal profession either here or in other countries, advised me that what I was about to embark on was madness. They assured me we'd probably lose at every contact during the battle. Late-night messages from Vancouver, concerned calls on my cellphone at dinnertime and a massive amount of anxiety in my own family made me even more nervous about how to proceed. The only people urging me to keep going were Eric and Dali.

They said that since this was such a public controversy, we should let the press have a copy of the letter over the weekend. While we have good relationships with many journalists, neither Rina nor I had it in us to 'leak' the papers. We felt it only right that M-Net have a chance to meet the deadline and duly respond. What I learned is that things don't work like that when it comes to love and war ... and I learned that from none other than M-Net. When they did eventually respond, instead of following what I understood to be the legal protocol – to lodge their response in court – they published it on their website – again, on a Friday night. But we'll get to that ...

News has a way of getting out, especially when there's a lot of public interest in a story. A reporter from eNCA heard that I was taking legal action and tracked down my attorney. Eric was interviewed on eNCA on the Sunday night and he confirmed that I was suing M-Net for R25 million and demanding reinstatement and compensation for defamation. And as Dali had anticipated, every headline the next morning was exactly that: 'Gareth Cliff Sues M-Net for R25 Million'.

The next day, on Monday 18 January, Eric was interviewed on 702 Talk Radio and announced that Advocate Dali Mpofu had been officially appointed as senior counsel and an urgent court application had been filed. The court date was secured for 26 January, just four days before the scheduled start of filming for *Idols* season 12. The wheels were turning.

As soon as Dali's name was revealed, a whole new wave of media interest broke. Quite apart from being a senior advocate at the Johannesburg Bar, Dali is also the national chair of the EFF, South Africa's youngest and most radical party. Their red berets, chants of 'Pay Back the Money' (#paybackthemoney) and outspoken and often controversial leader, Julius Malema, have become the most exciting thing on the political scene.

The next few days saw another media frenzy as the headlines went from 'Dali Mpofu to represent Gareth Cliff in Defamation Case' to 'Mpofu Representing Gareth Cliff Raises Eyebrows' to 'Dali Mpofu Criticised for Representing Gareth Cliff', 'Dali Mpofu Gets Tagged in Gareth Cliff Drama', and so on. The Twitter attacks on me were transferred to poor Dali, and I felt bad. Here was someone who completely believed in me and had my back, but who was subjected to nastiness on Twitter he really didn't deserve.

Dali is masterful and will remain one of my great teachers. When the EFF's Floyd Shivambu put out their statement, mostly condemning me as a racist and horrible human being, I admit that I found it confusing. I thought I had a good rapport with Julius Malema and I felt that I understood many in the EFF when it came to their disillusionment with the ANC and their passion for the good people of South Africa.

Julius and I have something of a parallel relationship. I've been called 'The white Julius Malema' for being outspoken and unapologetic, and he has often found himself likened to me for similar reasons. We both say what we think, and we often say what other people think, which means we make a lot of friends and enemies. In fact, he once said to me: 'There are people who don't like me and there are people who don't like you … But there are MORE people who like you and there are MORE people who like me.' Of course we would probably disagree on many things, but I think he's an extraordinarily passionate man with a great deal of charisma and influence. When we launched CliffCentral.com, Julius was my second guest, in an hour-and-a-half-long conversation that many people said was his best public engagement to date. He came out as eminently likeable and smart.

In its statement, the EFF said that they acknowledged Advocate Mpofu's professional right and obligation to represent whomsoever approaches and briefs him on any issue that relates to law, and that, in their view, professionals carry an obligation to provide any form of professional assistance to all people, irrespective of their race,

With Julius Malema

prejudices and background. They went on to say, however, that they 'hold a view that Gareth Cliff's defence of Penny Sparrow's racist remarks represents the worst form of racism. The EFF believes that Gareth Cliff is a racist, who holds white supremacist views consciously and sub-consciously.' They also brought up that notorious tweet about the late Health minister, Manto Tshabalala-Msimang, which was now being shared by Minister Mbabula and others to prove I was a racist. How could Dali wear both hats? I was perplexed.

When I asked Dali what he thought of this statement, he said it was just 'posturing' – I learned a great deal about posturing during this time. But he also said that this is exactly why we had to challenge the M-Net decision: their actions had opened me up to such 'unwarranted attacks' and 'knee-jerk labelling' and it would be good for us if it was raised in court by the opposition. And it was. It was used in court by M-Net's defence team to support their position of my being the poster boy for racism. They probably thought it would put Dali in a difficult position, but it played right into his hands.

I interviewed Julius on my show on CliffCentral a few months later and had the chance to discuss this with him. We both agreed that it's better for the racists to speak out so they can be identified. Because I'm white, it looked like I was supporting Penny Sparrow.

There were times when I was sure that this must be an episode of *House of Cards* and that Frank Underwood would appear at any moment.

M-Net Hits Back Hard

By Thursday that week, 21 January, M-Net had not met the deadline to respond, saying they would reply by Friday. But nothing came on Friday. Again, Friday night seems to have been chosen as the time for M-Net to release statements. At the same time as the responding affidavit was sent to Eric Mabuza, it was published on the M-Net website before being submitted to court. This was contrary to usual legal procedure, since these papers are typically first sent to the parties and the court before being published. These are the tricks that lawyers play, so I'm learning. It was, I suspect, aimed to intimidate.

M-Net hit back really hard. Two Fridays before, I had been axed from *Idols* for 'lacking empathy for the history of the country'; now

I was not only 'poison' but also the 'poster boy for racism'. Wow! Twitter was *lit* once again. By this time I had pretty much quit Twitter, but from what I'm told, 'Yolisa Phahle says Gareth Cliff is Poison' was the order of the weekend. By making their response public, M-Net's statement allowed a trial by Twitter before the matter was even heard in court. I don't know if I was feeling anything at this point, but I knew that I was not in a good place.

Even before M-Net responded, all sorts of well-meaning folk (some of them lawyers and some complete strangers) were coming forward with concerns. How can it be considered urgent by the court? It's just a TV show. How can you prove that you had been contracted if it's just a string of emails? What's Dali Mpofu's agenda? You'll never win against such a big corporation! Do you realise this will bankrupt you? If you pursue this, it will sink you and CliffCentral. They put the fear of God into me, and I'm not even sure which god I should have been afraid of. Some of our valued clients were being tagged on Twitter, which understandably scared them, and it was now beginning to impact negatively on my team and business.

Once the M-Net affidavit went public, it got worse. It's never nice to hear the unpleasant things said about you, much less in public, and exaggerated in order to justify the case against me. That's how court battles are played out – with acrimony. I had interviewed Yolisa Phahle just a couple of months earlier, and I was sure that the ugly things said about me didn't necessarily come from her. She's actually a gracious lady.

I was nevertheless close to withdrawing, no matter what the consequences so far might be. Rina picked up the phone and called Eric to ask him if we even stood a chance. I'm no stranger to controversy, but this felt more sinister than anything that had come before. We met with Dali and Eric over the weekend, and Dali pretty much said that I had come too far in my career and my commitment to South Africa to wimp out now. When I was worried about the potential costs, he said that if I didn't protect my reputation and let the Twitterari steamroll M-Net into firing me unlawfully, it would impact on any chance my business had of surviving. He was 100 per cent correct.

People don't understand free speech at all = Gareth Cliff is poison. That's a hell of a leap.

My Day in Court

Although I studied Law at the University of Pretoria, I never got the degree. Instead, I switched to History and International Politics, which I thought would be more fun. The idea of studying Law probably seemed enticing to me because people don't mess with you when you're a lawyer. You always need lawyers when horrible things happen – divorces, disputes, deaths, bankruptcies and crime. The truth is that most of the work a lawyer does is dreary administrative deskwork. The amount of time spent doing the things that TV law shows portray is a small slice of the life of even specialist litigators. I don't think I could ever have been as good as the best practitioners.

When you go through this kind of process, you sit with knots in your stomach. The costs of such an action are, for most people, out of reach. You have to let it all hang out, let the media pick up on every small detail of the kind that most people never share with anyone else, and give yourself over to the mercy of the court. Lawyers are adversarial and combative; they strategise, manoeuvre and bluff each other like great poker players, and you really have to trust your representatives, even if you're not sure you can afford to lose. In other words, you have to grow a big pair of brass balls.

When M-Net called me to that meeting in January 2016 to deliver the news that they wouldn't need my services for season 12 of *Idols*,

I walked out with an eye on the silver lining. I thought I was finally free of the last remaining tether to any kind of employer; I was in a very real way a free agent. CliffCentral.com was growing nicely, and I thought I could pour my heart and soul into it. Part of me was uncomfortable with the perception that I had been fired, and even more uncomfortable about the rumours about why I was fired, but I thought we'd muddle through and deal with problems as they arose. In retrospect, that might have been a dangerous move.

Dali Mpofu offered sage advice; he told me that the court is a great place to state your case, to stand up for what you believe in, and to clear your name. He also persuaded me that if you let poisonous monikers linger, they become the headlines in the story of your reputation. Of course he was right. I had to throw my hat in with him.

We had a small but powerful team: attorney Eric Mabuza, Senior Advocate Dali Mpofu – our nuclear weapon – and his juniors, Advs. Thembeka Ngcukaitobi and Frances Hobden. M-Net brought about 14 attorneys from Webber Wentzel, two senior advocates and a junior. Here was little old me, with our tiny media business up against mighty Naspers. The feeling that all those people in the court were there because of me was terrifying too; I was engaging the judicial system in a brazen way to assert my rights in a contractual dispute and I felt somehow guilty for taking up the court's time. It was intimidating, and I'm not even talking about the press in and outside the court, the noise and controversy on social media and the very uncomfortable feeling that I might let down some people I respected.

I don't know if you've ever been in a court of law, but there are all kinds of rules and traditions. A courtroom has an air of gravity and seriousness to it, not only because what goes on there has real-life consequences, but also because in this case there were so many people who were interested in what might happen. I chose to wear a blue suit because it's not as confrontational or sombre as black, but I decided to wear a tie so I didn't look too cavalier about the whole thing. There were reporters in the front, second and third rows, and Eric actually had to ask them to move up so I could find a seat. I sat behind my legal team and watched them sort through a mountain of paperwork, which made me even more nervous, but I tried not to let it show.

Attorneys wear suits in the High Court and advocates wear robes. The advocates' robes have a funny piece sewn on the back that traditionally used to be a pocket you'd put your money in when they represented you. They also wear little bibs and plain white shirts, and under the robes they have something called a 'dust-jacket', which is almost a jacket and almost a waistcoat. Senior advocates wear robes made of silk (that's why we call them 'Silks') and use the letters SC after their names. They also carry red bags to carry their robes when they're not in court. Junior advocates have blue bags and get paid less.

A lot of official buildings in South Africa have wooden wainscoting on the walls. During the apartheid era they discovered the ugliest way to apply the wood to the walls – usually in varying thicknesses of vertical planks, in a light-coloured, varnished hardwood. It has the effect of dampening sound and of making you feel that apartheid wasn't a great time for interior decorating. The High Court building in Johannesburg, as my sister warned me, is also famous for smelling of urine.

The judge, Caroline Nicholls, walked in and we all stood up. She bowed her head to us and we did the same to her. Then Dali Mpofu was on his feet, first placing on record that this case was not about racism as both parties were in agreement that I wasn't a racist, as M-Net had stated in their first press statement. He then meticulously went through the contractual issues, stating his case. It wasn't the most exciting thing I've watched, and if it hadn't been about me I might have nodded off a bit.

When Wim Trengove SC got up to argue M-Net's case I got a little worried. He has a larger-than-life reputation and was one of the advocates who successfully argued against the death penalty in *State* v *Makwanyane* in 1995. We had studied that case in our first year at law school. In fact, he was admitted to the Johannesburg Society of Advocates in 1975, before I was even born.

Advocate Trengove seemed belligerent, and said awful things about me (which wasn't my favourite part of the day), dismissing my contractual agreement with M-Net and slating my reputation. He added that *Idols* judges were hired to 'entertain, not shock and offend'. Judge Nicholls addressed this in her lengthy judgment, saying, 'It cannot be ignored that Cliff's value as an *Idols* judge has been his tendency to shock and provoke, an image that M-Net has apparently supported, or certainly overlooked, until now.'

Even worse, though, was when Oscar Pistorius was brought up. Advocate Trengove said that Oscar's sponsors had exercised their right to terminate their contracts with him because of his damaged reputation, which had the potential to tarnish their brands, and that the same should apply to me. Not only was I now the poster boy for racism who had supposedly tarnished my own reputation, but I was also being lumped in with a convicted murderer.

It took a lot of self-control for me to sit there and hear him say those things without reacting as I might in public. I'm used to hearing people say bad things about me – usually people who don't really know me and a few who are just nasty people – but it's hard to hear those things said in court where you can't explain yourself, and you have to let the lawyers do the talking for you.

Luckily, Dali got up after lunch and took over. He was passionate, vehement, unrelenting and persuasive. He took shots at Naspers, the parent company of M-Net, chastising them at their cheek in asserting that I lacked empathy for the country when their own record was abominable. He took pleasure in turning Trengove's introduction of the EFF's statement against him, and finished with the observation that 'This application might as well have been unopposed!'

The press gasped and chuckled. It was a *tour de force*, spurring him on to some scathing criticism of M-Net's case, their representation of me and their inability to stick to their own agreement. In a notebook I had taken to court, I wrote: 'Watching Dali at work, using words like "ridiculous", "absurd", "scraping the bottom of the barrel" was melodious. He's so adept and comfortable with confrontation that I thought fortune had smiled on me by bringing him in my hour of need.'

On Friday 29 January, Judge Nicholls took all of four minutes to read her finding into the record. The very detailed judgment (case number 1368/2016) was later made available, but at that moment all I remember hearing is: 'The contractual relationship has to be reinstated to what it was. M-Net will pay costs to Gareth Cliff.'

When I left the court with Rina, I felt like we'd fought a good fight. It wasn't about getting my gig back on *Idols*, and it wasn't only about setting the record straight with regard to my reputation. It was a fight for independent contractors who find themselves at the unfair end of contracts drafted by big corporations. It was about the important, free conversations our nation needs to have and that were stifled by the outrage of the Penny Sparrow debacle. And it was about showing the loudmouths on social media that I wouldn't be bullied, that I was *unfuckwithable*.

That night, in a familiar Friday night ritual, M-Net posted their response on their website and on social media:

M-Net statement: As ordered by the South Gauteng High Court, and as a good corporate citizen that respects the rule of law, M-Net will reinstate Mr Cliff as a judge on season 12 of *Idols* SA.

We believe we did the right thing by taking Mr Cliff off the show.

We remain committed to using our platforms to contribute to a
united South Africa.

(Whatever that meant. For the first time I was happy to be on the front
page of every newspaper the next day, with bold headlines proclaiming
this resounding win.)

Press Conference

The day after the judgment, the first round of *Idols* pre-auditions
started in KwaZulu-Natal and I held a press conference at CliffCentral.
com. Our little hub was bursting at the seams with CliffCentral contributors and journalists, fed with Krispy Kreme doughnuts. Outside,
the television broadcast vans set up for a live transmission of the event,
which I hosted with my lawyer, Eric Mabuza. Two weeks before, I had
held a meeting at the hub for all our presenters, just to keep them in the
loop. That had been in the middle of the firestorm. On this day, it was
most satisfying to demonstrate to people that everything CliffCentral
stands for had been reaffirmed.

At the start of the press conference, I read a statement that I had
prepared earlier with Dali Mpofu, who was already on his next assign-
ment in Port Elizabeth:

Welcome to CliffCentral. Thank you for joining us today.

*Yesterday Judge Caroline Nicholls ruled that my contract with
M-Net be reinstated and that I return to the panel on Idols. We've had
time to study the judgment in detail.*

*Before we begin, let me thank my team here at CliffCentral, my legal
team, the thousands of supporters on social media, and the many
people I have engaged with during this very challenging month. The*

thoughtful, useful discussions we have started to have in South Africa can only be good going forward ...

I'd also like to thank those people who stood up for me in the face of horrible allegations of racism, in the shadow of the despicable comments of Penny Sparrow and her like. In THIS country, with our history, we must remember how serious a thing racism really is. I repeat my apology to people who still feel that my statement on free expression was insensitive.

We welcome the statement issued by M-Net last night, confirming the court's decision to reinstate me, however I am concerned that they still insist they did nothing wrong. For ten seasons of Idols, I have had an excellent relationship with M-Net and the Producers of the show and in all that time this has been the only bump on the road. The road to reconciliation must always travel over the bridge of truth and I hope that one day M-Net will find it in their hearts to admit their mistakes as I have admitted mine.

Great people, people much more important than me – those who really suffered for our right to free expression, like Nelson Mandela – have said 'let bygones be bygones'. So who am I, a little ant compared to these giants, to hold a grudge? So I say 'let bygones be bygones' and the show must go on!

My only wish is that all South Africans, myself included, have learnt something from this episode. The month of January 2016 is ending tomorrow – it has been a difficult month for our country, since those idiotic, racist, hurtful and offensive remarks made by Penny Sparrow. As a country we now need to find the wisdom to make lemonade out of that bitter lemon.

If my High Court application and fine work of my attorney Eric Mabuza and Advocate Dali Mpofu and the rest of the team contributed a bit to ensuring that we end January 2016 in a better place than we started it, then it has been worth the sweat.

Thank you again to my colleagues, the legal team, my fellow South Africans and the founding mothers and fathers of our Constitution.

The debate on racism must be allowed to continue in an effective manner until we defeat those demons.

A very important correction I wish to make is that I dragged my fellow judges, Somizi and Unathi, into the matter. Nothing could be further from the truth. It was M-Net, in their statement of 9 January who brought them into it.

I quoted from M-Net's statement as to why I had been fired, and then continued:

Where to next? With regard to Idols, the show must go on! There are talented and not-so talented people lining up in Durban as we speak, waiting for their big break.

But here we are, in the CliffCentral.com hub – with so many of our amazing personalities here today – who together with us are building this platform that we launched in May 2014. This is about engaging in real conversations: about everything that happens in our world that we all experience every day – what makes us think ... laugh ... cry ... inspires us and empowers us.

This is now the platform where people don't have to be scared to have real, authentic and meaningful conversations – conversations that can foster greater understanding and unity in South Africa. We'll be leading the charge! We can and will continue to do what is necessary to build this great nation. If you haven't already joined our party, log on to CliffCentral.com, or download the CliffCentral app available on the Apple App Store and Google Play.

Viva #unscripted #uncensored #unradio Viva
Viva South Africa! Viva!

The floor was then opened for questions. After all we had been through, one question after another tried to fathom why I was in Johannesburg while auditions had apparently started in Durban. Did they start without me? Did I have a ticket to fly to Durban? Were they holding auditions up to wait for me? Had the ANCYL started their threatened protest? Had the other judges contacted me, etc. Besides some more thought-provoking questions from some of the CliffCentral hosts, the level of questioning was surprisingly superficial. Randall was evidently watching the presser on eNCA and caught sight of the Krispy Kremes. He sent a text: 'Make sure you bring some of those donuts with you on Wednesday.' That made me smile.

Eric Mabuza fielded the legal questions, and while he expressed our disappointment at the tone of M-Net's response, we were extending a hand of friendship and would likely not pursue the second part of our application – the defamation charge.

To this day, many people still think I won the money. Just between us, I didn't.

The Man in the Bin

The headlines in the newspapers over the next couple of days were pleasing. With the vast amount of publicity during this time, on top of everything else I really had to keep my head amid some really stupid reporting. The headlines were sometimes so decidedly odd that I wondered who gets paid to make up this stuff.

After the court ruling, the most featured photograph in the papers and social media, alongside the story of the win, was one of Dali and I walking down the street in front of the High Court, smiling, with a man rummaging through a rubbish bin on the side. Some of the captions that went with the photo were 'Gareth and Dali's victory dance' and Gareth and Dali 'celebrating' or 'walking triumphantly away'. What nonsense! Dali wasn't even at the High Court when the ruling was handed down. This photograph, taken by photographer Alon Skuy, was snapped at the beginning of the court case while Dali and I were on our way to the coffee shop, trying not to trip over the throng of press photographers running backwards in front of us.

On social media, on talk radio and in opinion pieces, people analysed, dissected and philosophised about the two contrasting South Africas – a 'rich' white guy and his advocate, and the poor man in the rubbish tip. eNCA even tracked him down and did a feature on him. He was 28 years old, and his name was Oscar Maile. The usual suspects weighed in, emphasising the socio-economic divide in South Africa, with many suggesting I take responsibility for the rubbish picker. Dali hit back against a tweet directed at him: 'Imagine if ALL the people faking concern for the guy were actually DOING something for his and others' economic freedom?'

The fact is that unemployment is a major problem in South Africa. According to the Statistics South Africa survey for the first quarter of 2016, Oscar Maile falls within the 26.7 per cent of the population that is unemployed. As many as 58.4 per cent of 18- to 29-year-olds have never worked before. That's a staggering statistic. South Africa once again was at the bottom of the pile among 140 countries measured in terms of its maths and science education, according to the 2015/16 World Economic Forum Global Competitiveness report. We came in 138th, with only Egypt and Paraguay ranked lower. Isn't that appalling?

For several years I have been involved with many of the Primestars education initiatives. Primestars Marketing, under the leadership of Martin Sweet, develops programmes for high school learners from disadvantaged communities, including maths and science, career guidance, financial literacy, leadership development and entrepreneurship. To date, some 200 000 secondary school learners have been reached

The infamous 'bin-man' picture, taken by Alon Skuy outside the High Court, January 2016.

nationally. The work is admirable and it's amazing to witness these thirsty young minds soak up these opportunities.

The bad news is that unless the economy grows, there just aren't any more jobs. The mining sector is in the doldrums, manufacturing is shrinking, the steel and textile industries have been overwhelmed by China, and even agriculture is employing fewer and fewer workers every year. The only thing that employs more and more people is government, and that doesn't grow the economy, just the tax bill. Since big corporations are too scared to argue with government or the unions, they act as accessories to the stagnant economy. Big businesses aren't growing and employing more people either, so that leaves just one thing to create employment in South Africa – small businesses. I don't think government, the unions or big business give a damn about small businesses; if they do, they have a funny way of showing it.

One of the reasons I'm so happy we started CliffCentral.com is that we're creating a few jobs, but, most importantly, we're also providing a platform to create content that informs, empowers, inspires and entertains. The internet represents a new way of doing things, a way to instantly connect and expose great ideas, products and services to huge markets. The internet, just as it will emancipate us through access to information and communication, will also provide the platform for the businesses of the future. Just last year, together with Virgin Atlantic, we helped the founders of two small businesses fly to London for Global Entrepreneurship Week, meet Richard Branson for a one-on-one meeting, and win cash prizes and marketing for their start-ups.

The 'third world' is actually the perfect place to discover the next big thing, because the opportunities to solve people's problems (which are significant here) are endless. We need reliable services, networks for trade and finance, technological solutions to diminish corruption and waste, and products that can make people's lives easier and more productive. Technology can help us solve many of these problems, and, in doing so, alleviate the burden of state control and big corporate influence on ordinary people's lives.

But, again, I digress …

Just a few weeks later, it was all about Pay Back the Money. Dali Mpofu and Wim Trengove once again walked into court together, only this time they were on the same side. That's how it works. This time it was the Constitutional Court and they were on the same side against the President. The EFF and DA took President Zuma to court for failing to uphold the Constitution and Advocate Trengove was representing the EFF.

As it was heard in court, President Zuma violated the Constitution and his oath of office over his treatment of Public Protector Thuli Madonsela's recommendations that he pay back some of the money spent on his home at Nkandla. This president of ours, who has weathered more storms and fought more battles than Moby Dick, has found himself almost constantly in some sort of trouble. This time it was serious. Chief Justice Mogoeng Mogoeng (so good you have to say it twice) delivered an eloquent and damning judgment of the President and thrust his fitness to hold office into serious question, perhaps even opening the doors for an impeachment.

Otherwise, it was business as usual back at *Idols* and the SJWs were trolling Twitter for their next victim.

Business as Usual

While our press conference was under way on that last Saturday in January, back in Durban the *Idols* hopefuls were lining up in the thousands outside the Playhouse Theatre for the first round of auditions. As I had to explain to the journos, the pre-auditions serve to sift through the crowd to select the best and worst singers to go through to the next round. Needless to say, the media were keeping a close eye, particularly because the ANCYL had said on TV the night before that I was a 'racist of the highest extremes' and 'anti-black', and that they would 'picket outside at the *Idols* auditions in Durban'.

Would the ANCYL be able to deliver this time? Apparently not. M-Net had appointed a head of public relations, Nondumiso Mabece (whom I hadn't met yet), who was quoted in one of the newspapers saying: 'We haven't seen anything aside from just the contestants coming through. We haven't had any disruptions. The crew has been here since 4 this morning and there was nothing. It's been a great day focused on talent.'

On the Tuesday night I joined my fellow judges and the producers on a flight to Durban and then for a leisurely dinner. ProVerb tweeted a group selfie and it was business as usual. So many people had predicted that the relationship had broken down beyond repair and this would be a difficult reunion. It wasn't. Nobody from M-Net was actually at the auditions, which is quite common, as it is the production company that delivers on the show. If the M-Net executives were holding out for something untoward happening, to prove their decision to dump me was correct, it didn't happen.

I had intended to stay out of the newspapers, but I was back in a matter of days. Young Nqobile Gumede of KwaMashu auditioned, and when Somizi delivered the bad news that she hadn't made it, she promptly fainted. Unathi rushed onto the stage and knelt down at her side. The paramedics arrived but it didn't look like much was happening so I got up to take her a glass of water. She was clearly out for the count and wasn't about to be sipping water from a glass. Since there wasn't a sign of a stretcher arriving, I instinctively lifted Nqobile up to take her to a better-ventilated area. There were some journalists attending the audition who were no doubt hoping to cover ANCYL protests outside the Playhouse, but instead, my carrying Nqobile out was the money shot. The photo was circulated far and wide in the newspapers and on social media, with many people now claiming that this proved I wasn't a racist. As much as I appreciated the sentiment, it was as ridiculous as labelling me racist for saying that people don't understand free speech.

When *Idols* started a few months later on Mzansi Magic, on 17 July 2016, it was like nothing ever happened. #IdolsSA was trending on Twitter before the show even aired. I wondered if the detractors would be back, but the excitement ahead of the 3 August election had evidently taken precedence. Bonisile from Tembisa hadn't forgotten and tweeted this:

Bonisile FromTembisa
@Bonisile_RMS

Thank you @AdvDali_Mpofu for fighting for Gareth so he can help carry unconscious girls on #IdolsSA! If he was fired who was gonna do it?

2016/07/17, 6:40 PM

Thanks Bonisile. Thanks Advocate Mpofu. Happily, Nqobile made a full recovery.

The auditions are a gruelling process for the contestants. Some of them travel long distances and line up from the early hours of the morning, often forgetting to eat or drink. After all the waiting, only a handful of people make it to the next round. I missed the Cape Town auditions as I was in Texas for the SXSW festival – that had been part of the discussion with regard to the contract in those now famous emails. Thank you to Jack Parow for standing in for me as guest judge. From Austin, Texas, I saw the next Twitter wave assuming that I had been dumped … again!

After many years at Sun City, *Idols* Theatre Week moved to the Wild Coast Sun this year. Theatre Week is probably the toughest time for the contestants. After the euphoria of making it through to the next round, the pressure is immense and the cuts brutal. The producers always come up with twists and turns that even come as a surprise to the judges. Once the top 16 are selected, our job as judges is mostly done. We then take a break as the producers edit the shows for the launch later in the year and the finalists wait it out until the live battle begins.

The Wild Coast is a lovely place, but it's a bit of a schlep to get there. Randall came down to breakfast the first day with a handful of some fizzy energy tablets, nothing he needed a prescription for, and he was complaining about the balcony. There was a notice next to the balcony door in his room warning that if you leave it open, baboons might come in and ransack your room. He found this unsettling. I suddenly had a vision of what the *Idols* judges would be like in the same old-age home, 40 years from now. We'd all be deaf from the bad singers, but we'd be laughing just as hard at all the old stories. I think we all deserve one of Randall's fizzy energy tablets.

After the auditions are over, every Sunday evening we're back at the

State Theatre in Pretoria for the live shows, where the finalists battle it out for the top spot. Once this has been decided, the judges can go home. It's now in the hands of the audience to choose the winner. After some performances, I sometimes wonder how some of our chosen ones even made it to the top 10, but in the end, the strong ones rise and new stars are born. I'm proud to have been part of such a successful show.

Many people had speculated that, after winning the court case, I would immediately resign just to make a point. Or, to be disruptive, I would start the season and then quit. It did cross my mind, but that would have been rather childish. At the end of season 12 of *Idols*, we took a trip to New York with the top four and ProVerb, and Rina and I arranged an appearance on Harry Connick Jr's new show, *Harry*. For a year that started with an actual judge reinstating me as a judge on *Idols*, we ended up on an *American Idol* judge's post-*Idols* show, ending things on an appropriate high.

My *Idols* journey ends here.

PART IV

My Wife: Unradio

'Entrepreneur: Someone who jumps off a cliff and builds a plane on the way down.'

REID HOFFMAN, FOUNDER OF LINKEDIN

Over the Cliff

What I am most proud of in my life so far is CliffCentral.com. Taking the plunge after a decade at 5FM was daunting but exhilarating at the same time. The only thing I can compare it to was the feeling of the bungee jump at Moses Mabhida Stadium in Durban – something I agreed to do for *Idols* while they were filming 'behind the scenes' at the Durban auditions. I instantly regretted it until the moment I jumped. Leaping into thin air is at the same time terrifying and euphoric. It's a rush.

That was really the only real risk I took during 11 seasons of *Idols*. As a judge, all I had to do was show up, be comfortably seated on the panel; the selected auditionees were brought out to perform in front of us. When we started CliffCentral.com we had our own auditions. Thousands of people queued up outside our little building from five in the morning in the hope of hosting a show. Black people, white people, old people, young people, people who were already in the radio business and total amateurs; people who were funny, boring, drunk and serious – it was the most experimental week of broadcasting in South African history. I remember one guy who reeked of brandy and had bloodshot eyes; he said he hadn't slept and wanted to do a show. He had been on his way to work as a dental technician and saw the queue and just decided to join it to see what might happen. I called him 'Solly the Drunk'. He was actually pretty entertaining, and slurred his way through a list of stories and answers to questions we threw at him.

Making the leap is one thing, but starting your own business is a long-term commitment, like getting married … and having children. As I watched all these people lining up while we were juggling so many balls, I wasn't even sure what shape it would take. It wasn't just about me any more; creating an internet platform was an opportunity for talented young South Africans to gain experience and grow their own brands. Many of our presenters, producers and guests would never have been given a chance in mainstream media and we're helping them to grow, organically. The internet represents new and interesting ways of doing things. This, I firmly believe, is the future. Several of these people went on to become part of the founding line-up of Touch Central just two years later.

'Entrepreneurship' is a popular buzzword these days; everyone talks it up and they all tell each other that being an entrepreneur is the best, shiniest and most exciting thing to be. As exciting as it is, entrepreneurship is more challenging than it sounds; there's a lot of anxiety, fear, impatience and frustration. The truth is that it's much, much easier to earn a salary, get your regular increases, fulfil a job description and budget accordingly. But the feeling of being unencumbered by 'damagement', and of being master of your own destiny, is worth it.

When we started CliffCentral, I was thankful that Rina Broomberg had been my manager for all these years and was there as co-founder. First of all, she has a wealth of experience – in management, in media, in people and in life. Although we would be sailing into uncharted territory, we were sure that we could attract an audience by offering unique new content, and could draw clients who were forward-thinking marketers. We knew we would be ahead of the curve, but that comes with being a pioneer.

The first thing I worked on was creating a manifesto, the kind political parties issue before an election, to let the electorate know what they want to do, and why you should vote for them. In March 2014,

I distilled my vision and values – energy, integrity and freedom – into what I call the Eight Commandments:

We will start something new to create happiness and laughter.

We will entertain each other.

We will raise the level of conversation and debate.

We will gather together positive, sincere people into our party, so we can talk and listen and get people thinking for themselves. We want people to know that they can take control of nothing until they take responsibility for themselves.

We will build a better vision for everyone than the politicians have. We don't need them. They can fuck off.

We will expand our freedom, and work against those who work with deceit and wield power cruelly.

We will engage in all of the above and exact only the absolute minimum of suffering from anyone else. We will hurt nobody.

We will fill up every day with great memories and experiences, and share a common future full of possibilities.

That's what we really care about.

That's what makes us passionate.

That's why we will make a difference.

I'm not the kind of guy who likes this sort of thing, especially when I see worker bees in big companies reciting it at company functions. That actually happened; I was the master of ceremonies at a big staff event to celebrate record profits, and the CEO made everyone stand up, as if they were in a Leni Riefenstahl movie, and recite the company values, aloud. I was horrified. Corporate culture (if there is anything resembling culture in a corporation) is something lived, not brainwashed into the people who make it work.

Yet here I was writing my own manifesto!

Building the Plane

Entrepreneurship was about to get real. My jets were fired but I had absolutely no idea of what to do. Jumping off the cliff was easy – now we had to build the plane. I had to keep my cards as close to my chest as possible, something that doesn't come easily for me. I usually blurt things out as they happen, which all too often gets me into trouble, but having a manager who is a veteran strategist helped enormously. It's at times like these that you learn to appreciate and value the friends in your life who you can really count on. None of my success would have happened without the extended team, which includes my loyal audience.

We took a handful of people into our confidence about the decision to leave 5FM. We needed a website and audio streaming for the new venture, which at that stage was just the kernel of an idea. The first person to be canvassed was Wayne Berger from iShack Digital, who hosted my website, garethcliff.com. We gave him some names to register the domain (none of which included my name) but they were all taken. While he was investigating, he sent a text to say that he had tried CliffCentral.com, that it was available, and that he had taken the liberty to register it in the meantime. It had a ring to it ... and so CliffCentral.com was born.

Our original premise to launch our new project was loosely based on the idea that, since it was an election year, we'd ride the campaign trail wave and 'launch' a political party that wasn't really political. Our show, and eventually our channel, would run as a candidate in the election. That idea may have had some merit, and I even sat up at home designing street posters into the early hours of the morning, but something even smarter was hatched. Rina was still consulting to ad agency TBWA Hunt Lascaris at the time. When we told them what we wanted to do, the brilliant minds at TBWA came up with something that was much, much better. And so 'unradio' was born: 'unscripted, uncensored … unradio – CliffCentral.com'.

A lot of ingredients have to be added to the pot at exactly the right time for it to make a good meal, and if Brett Loubser, CEO of WeChat, and marketing director Gerjo Hoffman weren't the kind of people they are, we might never have got things off the ground on the scale we did. It was a win-win. WeChat, which was establishing in South Africa at the time, is possibly the world's leading all-in-one mobile social communication app for smartphones. They had been an advertiser on my show on 5FM, and, after sharing our plans with them about building the first totally unrestricted, unscripted online platform, they jumped in and became our mobile partner for the launch. Our own dedicated app came after our first birthday as we evolved.

We had a website domain, a logo, a launch campaign and a sponsorship. What next? When I think back, it all makes sense now but I really had no idea how all this would pan out. Whatever happened, I was determined to make it work. After a chance meeting with Garry Hertzberg (who went on to host the *Laws of Life* show on CliffCentral), and mentioning our thoughts on online radio, he introduced us to someone he described as a 'technical genius' – Greg Cohen. Greg is a most unassuming and understated young man, but we knew he was the one person we absolutely had to have. He was our first employee and exactly what was required in a start-up – someone who could do everything. While Rina had encouraged me to take the risk to start my own business and be my own boss, she equally taught me that it's important to make yourself unnecessary to running the business: hire people who are smarter than you.

Many people questioned the logic of giving up a large listenership on national radio for a medium that attracts relatively tiny audiences by comparison, what with online radio being such a new concept in South Africa. Trust me, there were moments in the middle of the night when I woke up sweating, but once the decision was made I had no regrets at all. What I learned on this journey is that synchronicity and serendipity are more important than having a business plan. Our vision was to become the pre-eminent global content hub out of South Africa, and it's as though the universe conspired to help us.

The Comedy Central Experiment

After coming off a hugely successful breakfast show on 5FM, I did have concerns about Damon, Leigh-Ann, Mabale and I coming out of a computer and no one knowing where to find us online. That would have been rather lonely. How about having the show broadcast on a TV channel so everyone could see us? That made sense.

With that thought, we had a confidential meeting with the team from Comedy Central: CEO Evert van der Veer and marketing director Chris Torline. Comedy Central is a Viacom channel on DStv that airs international programming and local comedy, including the famous roasts. We'd had discussions with them previously, but this time we suggested the idea of hosting a live radio show on TV. The ratings at that time of the morning were surely small enough to take a risk.

It was a complicated thing to get right: the live TV/radio studio had to beam the transmission to London and then back to South Africa via satellite, we had to take timed commercial breaks, and we had to, for the first time, think about the show from a visual point of view. It was a bold idea, and one that nearly drove me crazy. There was the question of which part of the show should be chosen for TV, and how different it should be to the rest of the show, which I intended to be conversational, rather than full of gimmicks and features. TV is produced in segments, not as a whole. Radio is different. Instead of just having Damon talking in my ear while I was trying to make sense and keep the show entertaining, I now had a TV producer counting down and telling me when to come in. Remember, this was all done live, with no rehearsals and with real-time trial and error. I'm surprised any of us survived, but we did and pulled off the launch without a single hitch.

To Comedy Central's credit, they supported us 100 per cent and were extremely generous with branding – from the elaborate backdrop to co-branded mugs and mouse pads. They really did want this to work. The backdrop, however, was another bone of contention. There was little time to spend on design, and what looked good on paper was terrifying for me when it was mantled the night before launch. Splashed behind me was 'The Gareth Cliff Show' in HUGE letters on a busy background. While it did show the audience that we were a real radio show with a state-of-the-art studio, it reinforced the perception that I had merely moved my radio show to Channel 122 and detracted from the fact that we were in the process of establishing some 35 shows across the CliffCentral.com channel.

Another reason I wanted to do something new and get out of radio was because of the formatting, the endless interruption of commercial breaks and the time restrictions. Now, because of this simulcast TV and radio project, I found myself too stressed about hitting the time markers and what we looked like on screen to deliver the kind of content I had imagined we'd do. This was not the liberating experience I had envisioned for us at CliffCentral.com. When the decision to cancel the TV simulcast was taken, I was relieved. In retrospect, we could have kept going and it might have become successful, but I think we were trying too many things for the first time, all at once. That did not end our relationship with Comedy Central. Later that year, I hosted the show *Divine* and I have no doubt we will do other projects together in the future.

Needless to say, the press had a field day, relishing the fact that I had 'failed'. On the contrary, the Comedy Central experiment was a valuable lesson on the pioneering path. It served as a vital part of our launch and helped us to clarify our primary identity as an online content hub. The biggest advantage to being on television when we launched was in showing the world that we were a full-fledged operation and not just me broadcasting from my laptop in my garage. The downside was that many people thought we were just a TV show and didn't know about the other 11 hours of the day in which we were already creating amazing new content.

We could now focus our energy again. Despite the challenges of getting the audience to try streaming or podcasting for the first time, we went back to trailblazing online content.

The Team

Leaving a company where you've been for many years, as dysfunctional as it may be, is like leaving home. When I was thinking about the move from 5FM, I was most concerned about my team, who had become my radio family – executive producer Thabo Modisane and 'Thabo's Assistant' Damon Kalvari, news anchor Leigh-Ann Mol, trafficologist Mabale Moloi, sports coach Sias du Plessis, Hollywood reporter Jen Su and our young intern, Siya Sangweni-Fynn. Management had already indicated that, if I decided to leave, there wasn't necessarily a future for them.

This is what made the decision so difficult for me. While I was taking a risk, I didn't want to put them at risk. In fact, I almost stayed on at 5FM just so they wouldn't lose their jobs. While they knew I might leave, I had to keep them in the dark until two weeks before the big announcement, when I told 5FM, but they didn't hesitate to make the decision to come with me. Sias was offered the afternoon sports slot on 5FM, so it was understandable that he opted to stay, because he has a wife and child to support. Thabo, who's not a risk-taker at all, got cold feet on the last day of the show. Fortunately 5FM managed to find a shift for him, so he was safe.

Damon, Leigh-Ann, Mabale, Jen and Siya were the founding members of CliffCentral.com. Damon perhaps had the hardest time; his wife thought it was going to be a disaster. She warmed to the idea only when we had a strategy session with WeChat at the Radisson Hotel. If we could afford the Radisson, she must have thought, then we were maybe onto something.

Leigh-Ann Mol didn't even blink at the fact that she was leaving 5FM after 15 years. She left CliffCentral a few months later to hook up with business journalist Lindsay Williams, who almost joined us. Lindsay and I had first worked together at 702, and he would do our wacky business reports on 5FM by phone from Cape Town. I had introduced him to Leigh-Ann on one of his visits to Johannesburg, and soon a romance started to blossom.

Lindsay had worked on 2oceansvibe, the country's first real online station (there was also Ballz Radio, which was started by Darren Scott after he was fired from Jacaranda for using the k-word at a staff function). I had been approached by 2oceansvibe two years earlier about joining them, but I felt it was still much too soon for online radio. In making the decision to start CliffCentral.com, I believe we were also ahead of the curve but a little closer than 2oceansvibe when Seth Rotherham started it in 2010. Seth was certainly a visionary. Lindsay gave us some valuable input and would have liked to play more of a business and strategic role in my start-up, but, quite frankly, at that stage I even wasn't sure exactly what I was starting up! That story does have a happy ending though. It was sad to lose Leigh-Ann when she followed her heart to Cape Town and Lindsay, but what's better than a love story that ends happily ever after, right?

The only person who was actually safe was Siya the intern. That's because I – not 5FM – was paying him. Siya had entered our lives a couple of months earlier – on Twitter! He had been in matric the previous year at Westville Boys' High and wanted to take a gap year to explore the entertainment world. Being a proactive kid, he contacted everyone who was anyone in the industry, but didn't get much of a response. How he found Rina on Twitter I'm not quite sure, but he struck gold – Rina has an eye for spotting talent and always responds to a bright spark. We met him in January, by then with his matric in hand, and agreed to take him on as an intern for our business, One on One Productions (the company from which CliffCentral.com was born). We warned him that he would be witness to one of the greatest radio upheavals in the next few months. We agreed to the internship on condition that he began his tertiary studies the following year, and we committed to sponsoring his education. He in fact became the first student of what we call the 'CliffCentral Campus', and his gap year turned into two years.

I missed Sias and Thabo. I missed having a guy who could talk about guy things. Siya was still a baby and Damon was Damon. Ben Karpinski is another long-time friend and award-winning sports blogger. When he showed an interest, I didn't hesitate. The team was complete. Ben with the big head was on board.

What I learned about starting a new venture is that the fuel comes from the enthusiasm of those around you. Arye Kellman also left 5FM to join us with no promise of any payment or job description. His initial work on my show was outstanding, but he distinguished himself by helping to run the auditions in a very quirky, original way. It was half interview, half therapy session, and he got people to open up about their lives, loves and feelings. We decided he needed a permanent daily show to benchmark the end of the day, like my show would at the start. Arye, despite some experience in radio, was the first real podcast broadcaster in South Africa. He, together with his producer, Katleho Molai, and contributors, share human experiences and stories from the millennial perspective, with the aim of trying to make sense of a generation that is trying to make sense of itself. With the launch of Touch Central, Arye and producer Kat, as well as Katlego Mahoaduba and Oneal Madumo, two of our first auditionees, went on to land prime-time slots on the new channel. This is what it's all about – drawing up the blueprint for a new kind of medium, creating new opportunities and, with that, finding a new way to bring sponsors and advertising into the mix.

You know you're doing something right when so many people want to join you, even though none of us knew what it was yet. We agreed with a handful of them that they could volunteer for the first month, having no idea what they would actually do. They ended up doing everything from processing the hundreds of auditions, making coffee and handing out water to emptying dustbins and piling up chairs. Some of these people later became staff members, and each one had their own story of what brought them to our doorstep.

And then there's Jane … Everybody loves Jane. Rina's domestic worker, Jane Malatji, came twice a week to help with the cleaning. She's not the greatest cleaner, but is a character in her own right and has since joined full-time, being not only the most gracious host for our guests but also a charming production assistant for the shows. That's what CliffCentral.com was always meant to be about – a place where people could learn and grow.

As we grew and serendipity continued to play its part, Neil Meintjes, another childhood friend of mine, who had more experience in the digital world than I did, came up with a proposal to connect content with clients. And so the sales department was born. We also received calls from many high-profile people working at other radio stations who were more than ready to jump ship. The only two people we did eventually hire were from Primedia; Rina had employed both of them 15 years earlier when she was the MD of 702. Dori van Loggerenberg became our content manager and Tanya Surat our sales superstar. Dori and Tanya brought experience, bearing in mind that virtually everyone else started as an intern and was under 25. It was also a good feeling reuniting with colleagues from my early days at 702 and creating a new media future together.

Sometimes in life it's about being in the right place at the right time and having the chutzpah to show up, even uninvited. That was true for Michael Flax. He was always hanging around during those early days, and neither Rina nor I had a clue who he was. We assumed he was part of the Comedy Central technical crew because he was often in the production booth helping them, or that he was an auditionee who never left. There was no security, so anyone could come in or out. We didn't want to get to know him because we knew his days would be numbered once the TV experiment ended. After the second month, when the TV crew had packed their cameras away, 21-year-old Michael Flax was *still* hanging around. It turned out he had followed Arye Kellman into the building and had quietly blended in. Where there's a will, there's a way. So Flax became an 'honorary' intern, and quietly entrenched himself as my full-time producer some months later when Damon Kalvari left to pursue his own entrepreneurial efforts as a perfume-maker.

Most important was our core group of listeners, who were there to support us from the start. When I left 5FM, no one knew what we were planning, but some listeners caught on immediately. Just after I made the announcement at 6 am on 31 March 2014, @ThembaNtleki tweeted: '@GarethCliff can you start your station online. It can just run from 6–9 weekdays :(#RadioIsDead.' Themba is sharp; he found

CliffCentral turns one! With the founding family, 2015.

the CliffCentral.com app while it was still in test phase, before any-one else even knew about it. Themba was one of the early adapters I was relying on to chart this new territory with us. CliffCentral.com quickly became a thriving community, with fans engaging with us on the shows and on social media. Two of them, Cindy from Ireland and Mfundo from Durban, even flew in to celebrate our first birthday with us. 'Superfans' like Cindy and Mfundo keep us on our toes and tell us when we need to take things up a level. I love you all!

Even Dogs Allowed

CliffCentral.com had a lot of personality from the start. Actually we had multiple personalities. In our first week, we decided to launch my show, followed by rolling auditions from 9 am to 6 pm. We didn't really know what kind of 'line-up' we'd end up with, and we weren't sure whether podcasts would be a big or small part of the offering. We were figuring it out as we went along.

Holding auditions was one thing, but there were famous people like Casper de Vries who weren't being seen or heard on any other channel at that time. Casper is one of South Africa's gems, but his outspoken views on religion, language and politics have pissed a lot of people off. He is multitalented, being an actor, comedian, entertainer, painter,

Casper de Vries and his dogs, Halfrieda and Kent, pre-launch at CliffCentral, April 2014.

composer, director and producer. He had been one of my last guests on 5FM, and I invited him to come and do a show on CliffCentral. With Casper came his dogs, Halfrieda the Alsatian and a crossbreed mutt called Kent. Like their master, Halfrieda and Kent are energetic and quirky, and they quickly made themselves at home. They were received with mixed reactions. On encountering Halfrieda, one of the auditionees had a panic attack, and one of our interns would hide in the production booth when the dogs were visiting. Dog hair was lovingly left on the couches and all over the studio, with the result that two staff members developed allergies. Nevertheless, Kent and Halfrieda earned their place as part of the CliffCentral.com founding family, and Casper's weekly show quickly became the top downloaded podcast.

Trevor Gumbi, another all-round entertainer in comedy and on TV, also joined the ranks with co-host Gabi Mbele. He too truly tested the boundaries of this new 'uncensored' and 'unscripted' platform. Their show was called *TG-Squared* and started with the line 'Make Monday Your Bitch'. It certainly kicked off the week in the most raucous manner imaginable. There's a window between the studio and the production area, so Trevor could assess the cringe levels. The more he saw looks of disbelief, the more risqué he would become. Trevor was also one of the first guests I interviewed on my CliffCentral show, and he opened up about not having a father, suffering sexual molestation and being the target of bullies at school, and later on about his cocaine addiction. He dealt with all this by making jokes, and so comedy became his happy place. In fact, what I have loved most about the CliffCentral journey is the range of people I've interviewed and how they've shared the most incredible stories.

As much as we weren't censored, there was a lot of internal discussion as to how far you could go before you start to self-censor. That was something I never wanted to do. I too enjoyed this newfound freedom and also swore a lot on air, played all the clips and songs I couldn't play on 5FM and revelled in being emancipated. This is probably the thing Rina and I fought most about in the early days. She felt that just because we're uncensored, we shouldn't have to become ungovernable. I don't have many vices, but I do swear. I think swearing is now commonplace. Rina still berates me for using the f-word on the show, but, let's face it, four-letter words have been around for centuries. As much as parents won't want to admit it, it's also part of their kids' vocabulary from an early age. I read an article in *Time* magazine by a psychology professor, Timothy Jay, who reckons that by the age of two most children know at least one swear word. Some people would say that people who swear lack vocabulary. It's not that at all. Sometimes it's just so much more satisfying to say 'Fuck off' than 'Please leave'.

We had a good balance, though. Other shows that fell into place during the first few weeks were a mix of well-known personalities and complete newcomers. Some of the founder shows included well-known celebrities such as Tumisha Masha, Hlubi Mboya and Penny Lebyane, business leaders such as Adriaan Groenewald and Ellis Mnyandu, and a range of new presenters hosting shows on celebrity gossip, technology, youth panels, education, entrepreneurship, health, love and relationships – everything that was relevant to our audience. Central to all the shows was one of our volunteers, Duncan Mabaso, who went on to become the studio coordinator and an integral part of those teams.

The fact that we could do anything in these shows – there were no prohibitive rules, no bulletins of sport, formal news or irrelevant traffic, no boring weather reports and no commercial interruptions – meant that the content could become a satisfying and distilled value proposition to the audience. This gave us complete freedom to pioneer amazing, original South African content.

We had some interesting neighbours during the first year. Our studio is in the greater Telemedia complex, which mostly houses television studios. It wasn't long after our launch that the Oscar Pistorius trial started, and that in itself made broadcasting history. DStv Channel 199 set up shop directly opposite our studio for 24/7 Oscar television coverage. 'The Oscar Pistorius Trial – A *Carte Blanche* Channel', as it was called, scored record ratings across the board.

The Oscar trial saw many twists and turns, from his being convicted for culpable homicide to having that overturned to murder. Like most people, I was prone to jumping to the finish line and proclaiming Oscar guilty or not guilty. I knew Reeva Steenkamp. I didn't know her well, but she came to two of my birthday parties and once showed my mother how to use a new dishwasher. She was a friend of one of my ex-girlfriends, and she and my brother were briefly interested in each other (I think, but don't want to speculate). I also knew Oscar. Well, I interviewed him once or twice and bumped into him occasionally at parties and events. I didn't like or dislike him. We never swapped numbers or invited each other to anything, so I'd be lying if I said we were anything but shallow acquaintances.

The whole tragic episode made me think about our celebrity culture. I'm suspicious of hero worship. I think we mammals do a pretty awful job of living up to our ideals of greatness and perfection. More and more on social media, we see people elevated by popular acclaim and then delight in seeing them brought crashing down again. Politicians, sports stars, celebrities and entertainers are all fair game.

The Oscar saga was a sad state of affairs, but the biggest advantage of having Channel 199 on our doorstep was easy access to the variety of guests who came in to appear on the TV panels. We could direct them to our studio for a quick interview and have our own coverage. We were happy when it was over, though. We got all our parking back.

Tech Paradise

With CliffCentral.com my obsession and the exciting world of tech start-ups and content my new playing field, I wanted to make the second year of this new project even more exciting than the first. I had the good fortune to enjoy, in the space of three months, both a phenomenal, eye-opening trip to the South by Southwest (SXSW) festival in Austin, Texas, and, only a month and a half later, a tremendous excursion to Silicon Valley, outside San Francisco.

Anyone who knows anything in the world of tech will tell you that if you're in San Francisco or Austin, you're at the heart of the new economy. Both of these cities have established themselves as the addresses of some of the world's biggest companies (Google, Facebook, PayPal, WhatsApp, Apple, Cisco Systems, Intel, etc.) and as focal points for innovation and futurism.

Brett Loubser of WeChat, the guy who had in so many ways made it possible for us to start CliffCentral.com on the level we did, invited me to SXSW. He takes his team there every year because he thinks it's the most important tech convention in the world. He's right. The part of the convention we went for was called 'Interactive', and featured keynote addresses from JJ Abrams (the film director, screenwriter, producer and composer, most famous for *Star Wars: The Force Awakens*), Kerry Washington (who plays Olivia Pope in *Scandal*) and Barack Obama. Yes, SXSW, or South-By, as regular attendees call it, is now important and mainstream enough to attract a sitting president of the United States of America.

Never mind the tech extravaganzas, do you know how good the tequila is in America? You see, I don't drink beer or any other spirits. I'll sometimes have wine with civilised people at dinner, but I really only drink tequila, and since I don't imbibe any other substances, I sometimes overdo tequila, but never to the point of disgrace. There are three kinds of tequila: *blanco, reposado* and *añejo*. *Blanco* is clear and comes straight from two distillation procedures into the bottle as 'silver' tequila. It kicks like a mule and isn't my preferred variety. *Reposado* is 'gold' tequila, and has been resting (reposing) for between two and twelve months in a barrel. This is good, but not very special. It'll do. The third variety, *añejo* (meaning 'aged' or 'vintage'), a dark gold or brown colour, is as smooth as the best whisky and should be sipped in a sophisticated way, rather than smashed down your throat from a shot glass. Tequila is made from a marvellous plant, the agave, which produces only one rosette of flowers and then dies. Such is the sacrifice nature makes to bring us this terrific stuff, and I will be grateful for all eternity. Texas has some amazing tequila bars, and the best selection you could imagine.

Back to the convention. In Austin you see a lot of strange stuff. The city motto is 'Keep Austin Weird', and they work hard to keep it that way. It's a very liberal, hippy, friendly place – not like the rest of Texas, which is a lot like the TV show *Dallas*. I walked past a poster that showed a young woman with short hair and pretty eyes, and where her mouth was meant to be there was an ugly, hairy asshole. That's the kind of thing you see everywhere in Austin. There's a lot of eating, but there's also a lot of brain food. Everyone was talking about virtual reality, robots and artificial intelligence. I saw a robot that could solve a Rubik's cube in 15 seconds, a 3-D printer copying Lego bricks and the latest drone that can fly to a point on the map, take photographs while hovering over a location and come straight back.

Everyone in Austin (and in Silicon Valley, I later discovered) isn't really there. They're a few years in the future, but their bodies are here in the present. Invariably, you find that a lot of conversations are about what humans will do when robots do all the work, how we could live forever and what your fridge might tell your watch or tablet. It's a little weird, but you get to like it.

A few weeks later, I was heading back to the USA, this time to Silicon Valley. I had been invited by En-novate (a venture co-founded with Investec), along with 22 other South African tech entrepreneurs, to visit the very epicentre of the world's most innovative, disruptive tech businesses. It was a whirlwind itinerary of meetings, workshops and experiences. The idea behind the trip was that the benefits would spill over into businesses in South Africa.

The whole trip was an eye-opener, but the highlight was meeting Roelof Botha, a partner at venture capital firm Sequoia Capital, and possibly the most powerful South African in Silicon Valley. Sequoia's start-up investments have grown businesses that now command 22 per cent of the tech-heavy Nasdaq stock exchange. We waited in Sequoia's austere, uncluttered boardroom for Roelof, who was the youngest actuary to qualify from UCT and a man who can speed-dial Elon Musk, Reid Hoffman and just about any other billionaire on the West Coast. He spoke to each of us with absolute focus, took every question as seriously as if it was about his own personal interest and remained friendly and helpful to everyone. If I learned anything from Roelof, it was that the basics of human connection and conversation remain the most fundamental tools, whether you're seeding the next giant tech business, or talking to someone on the street.

If you want to be the next big thing, and you want to make lots of money, find a problem that many people have, and solve it for them. Using technology to create solutions for humanity is where all the big success stories of the next decade or two will come from. No government, trade union or South African bank will be able to do things as fast or as well as someone with a good idea and the determination to do great things. No government tender will make you nearly as rich as a great idea with exponential growth and vision. Being at the southern tip of Africa doesn't mean you can't run with the big dogs – just ask Elon Musk or Roelof Botha.

Another happy realisation was the flexibility that came with having an online radio show. You can broadcast from anywhere in the world. I was able to Skype in to the show every morning and share my stories, as they were happening, with the audience at home.

The internet is a global meeting place. Status and influence are now measured in likes, followers, retweets, downloads and Klout scores. Even those who have plenty of material wealth and political status crave these new accoutrements of rank. Royals, cabinet ministers and billionaires compete with reality TV contestants, evangelical preachers and porn stars to trend. This really is an exciting time to be alive!

From Infant to Toddler

The first year of CliffCentral went by in the blink of an eye ... and so did the second. When we launched on 1 May 2014, I decided to have my family as my inaugural guests. Although I have tried to keep my family away from the heat of all the publicity, noise and nonsense over the years, I decided it was only fair to acknowledge the people who have been there from the start of my life and who have supported me every step of the way. They are the ones who keep me grounded.

I love my parents. My dad, Rory, is strong and principled, sometimes to a fault. He loves his children and would move mountains for us – and I know how worried he was about my taking such a big risk with CliffCentral and with the *Idols* court case. My mom, Monica, is the glue in our family. She puts everyone else first and is the one to reel us in if we get ahead of ourselves. When CliffCentral.com was born, my parents were joined in the studio by my brother, Robert, and his wife, Skippy – with their two-month-old baby, Luke – my sister, Sandra, and my dog, Carl.

Reaching our first birthday was psychologically an important milestone for all of us. To mark the occasion, I invited the most influential, most resolute woman in South African society – the Public Protector, Advocate Thuli Madonsela – for an hour-and-a-half interview. For the first time, we also video-streamed the interview, launching 'unTV', just as we had pioneered unradio. You can still see the recording, which went out live, on YouTube.

As many people already know, Thuli is a soft-spoken and thoughtful person. She's not the one who drops one-liners the non-thinking media like to reproduce as headlines. She doesn't make great soundbites, she makes solid sense, and as a result the very important things she says and does are often glossed over. This is a great pity, not just because (as many of her adversaries aver) she is critical of government and the governing party, but because her work must be done in rigorous, pain-staking ways in order to produce findings that uphold the interests of all South Africans against a powerful opponent – the government.

After the interview, Thuli stayed to celebrate our birthday and took time to engage with our staff. I felt honoured to have her there to share this milestone, and I'm sure I'll be prouder still when, long after both she and I are gone, history gives her the recognition she deserves for upholding the values of our constitutional democracy.

In another blink our second birthday was upon us. My nephew is just a couple of months older than CliffCentral.com. I have observed him and some of his friends and have found that two-year-olds are bright-eyed, energetic and unafraid. They push the boundaries to see how much their parents will let them get away with, and they absorb every-thing like a sponge. All of these things are equally true of our young content business. In the space of the last two years, we have disrupted the media industry, made tremendous strides in writing the blueprint for a new kind of online hybrid podcaster/broadcaster, forged some incredible partnerships and created some of the best original content South Africa has seen in many years.

CliffCentral's first birthday, with Thuli Madonsela and Rina Broomberg, 2015.

In our formative years, we've had groundbreaking conversations about the things that affect all South Africans. We have become a voice of social media on the one hand, and a truly independent media platform on the other, with a show for every taste and interest.

We've passed all the milestones we laid out at the start of this venture, and I have no doubt that the future is ours. I'm particularly proud of the great audio archive of the South African patchwork quilt that we're building; it will be a time capsule of the unique tales that weave us together and will remind us of how far we've come.

Touch Central

Success comes from consistently improving and inventing. With CliffCentral.com running like clockwork and growing nicely, the next leap was imminent. And what was to come was yet another channel – Touch Central. Again, serendipity played its part.

If you've read through the book in sequence so far, you will have gathered by now that, as public as my life may appear, I tend to be a bit of a recluse. My favourite place to be is at home. I rarely go out and, unlike the Gareth who used to go to the opening of an envelope in his twenties, you'd have to be very special to get me to attend a society event now. I say this not to appear full of myself, but rather because that kind of small talk and air-kissing is something I'm actually not good at.

When Carolyn Steyn invited me to her birthday party, I knew I had to go. First of all, she's a lot of fun, and second, besides her theatre background and celebrity status, she does really good work. She launched 67 Blankets for Mandela Day, which has become something of a movement. In 2016, the *Guinness World Records* officially recognised their successful attempt at creating the world's biggest blanket. The birthday party in question was a lavish but not overly grand event. There were a number of prominent businesspeople, some very powerful politicians and the cream of the social scene – and Fikile Mbalula, the Minister of Sport, whom the media had recently dubbed my 'nemesis'.

Naturally, Fikile was the first person I went to say hello to. We greeted each other warmly enough for two people who had been 'twarring' with each other. I called him 'Minister' and he called me 'Garath'. We talked for a while and joked about Twitter and how so many people overreact to what goes on there. Then we posed for a picture with Anele Mdoda, which circulated on Twitter. The poor mob on Twitter were so confused that I'm sure some of them got no sleep. It seems that in the minds of so many on social media everything is totally binary. It's not on to have any complex or nuanced relationships or opinions.

Anyway, the main reason I'm telling you about the party has to do with someone else – Thabo (Tbo Touch) Molefe. Despite working in the same building, right across the foyer from each other, at the SABC for about eight years, we'd never really had a conversation. While I was doing the breakfast show on 5FM, he was hosting afternoon drive on Metro FM. I had heard people gossip about him and his American twang and his VIP friends and connections, but I knew nothing about him. We lived in different worlds.

I learned a lot more about Thabo Molefe, known as 'Touch', over the next few weeks. He was born in Sharpeville and raised by his grand-parents, Dr PF and Rose Ntombiyokuthula Molefe, when his parents went to America with their church. His entrepreneurial spirit started flourishing from an early age. He founded an entrepreneurs' club in school, and at age 15 he was already flying international acts such as Monifah and Foxy Brown into the country. Touch relocated to America in 1997 where he was adopted by the famous Bishop Robert Jones (brother of singer and actress Grace Jones) and his wife, Majorie, and finished his schooling and university studies in New York. His career on Metro FM in fact started out of New York in 2004. He convinced Lesley Ntloko, head of radio at SABC, to have a satellite studio in New York and possibly host a radio show live. The deal was sealed and Metro FM went live with Tbo Touch from New York City every Saturday between 8 and 9 pm. After he came back to South Africa, he went on to dominate the afternoon drive-time slot and expanded his showbiz influence.

At the time of the party, Touch was thinking of leaving Metro FM, a move that would be a big loss to that station. He's had his share of controversies and suspensions and, as a boundary-pusher, was feeling increasingly stifled. We naturally had a conversation about what was next, and I explained how empowering and liberating it has been to work for myself and create CliffCentral.com.

The penny dropped instantly – Touch's brain turns into something of a lightning conductor when a great idea lands. Sparks fly in all directions. For about an hour, we schemed and thought out loud about what kind of operation he could launch. Shortly afterwards, he resigned from Metro amid much publicity. There was a huge stir on social media and in news headlines after his resignation letter circulated on Twitter. This was on the same day that Acting CEO Jimi Matthews resigned from the SABC. It felt like the SABC was crumbling in front of our eyes. At the time, Touch had just wrapped up production on the historic Jazz Epistles concert featuring Abdullah Ibrahim, Hugh Masekela and Jonas Gwangwa, which brought together former presidents Thabo Mbeki and Kgalema Motlanthe, Deputy President Cyril Ramaphosa and EFF leader Julius Malema under one roof for the performance. Despite all the drama at the SABC, no one saw Touch's resignation coming.

We started exploring the possibility of a whole channel called Touch Central. After a few more meetings, late-night calls and quick decisions, Touch flew off to America to tie up some deals and opportunities. When he landed back in Johannesburg, we wasted no time in planning the announcement, logo, line-up and launch for the same week. It all happened so fast that my head is still spinning, but that's how we roll ...

Just a few days before the municipal elections, while the political parties were still scrapping for control, we formed our own coalition. Touch Central (TouchCentral.fm) was born, the first 24-hour-a-day online radio station, with CliffCentral.com continuing as the podcasting king. The launch was arranged in true Touch style. On 29 July 2016, a crisp winter's morning, Tbo Touch and his team arranged a press conference, dubbed 'Touch on Air', in which journalists and celebrities were hoisted 50 metres into the air around a five-star dining table. It was in the air that Touch and I announced the launch of a 24-hour online music channel ... free from censorship, free from restrictive formats ... free to be ... the underlying philosophy that cemented our partnership.

Touch Central is born, with Tbo Touch, 1 September 2016.

On 1 September 2016, Touch Central went live. All the experience and hard work from the previous two years of building CliffCentral. com enabled us to move in record time to launch Touch Central with a powerful line-up and smart new app, ushering in this next level of on-line entertainment. Tbo Touch, in particular, made a grand entry for his first show, accompanied by Jessica Motaung and the Kaizer Chiefs team. Social media and the phone lines went crazy. *Your boy* Touch was back.

#DataMustFall

It's unlikely that anyone would have predicted a partnership between Tbo Touch and me. They say the best scenario for a successful start-up is for the founders to be as different as possible. Touch and I are completely opposite in every way. His team is Kaizer Chiefs and I support Sundowns. He has Joyous Celebration performing on his Monday Replenishment while I have Soweto Gospel Choir singing my jingles. His show is music-driven while mine is mostly talk. He is a man of God while I'm a man of science. I'm comfortable wearing no-name brands while Touch is always dapper and bedecked in designer labels. My idea of a good meal would be a tomato and avo salad at home while he dines in the finest restaurants. No one would recognise my friends in the street; his are among the most high-profile celebrities and politicians in South Africa and even abroad. He brought in an investor for Touch Central; I brought an infrastructure. Touch is the accelerator while I am the brake.

What a year 2016 turned out to be. From the lows of Penny Sparrow and the *Idols* court case to the trip to Silicon Valley and the launch of a second channel. It was exhilarating and downright bizarre. But there was more to come ...

On the afternoon of 20 September, I found myself sitting next to Tbo Touch in the Old Assembly room of Parliament. Our business was less than a month old and we had been invited by the Portfolio Committee on Telecommunications and Postal Services to make a presentation on the cost of communication and data. In the wood-panelled chamber, with its green leather seats and elaborate carvings, sat two of the youngest entrepreneurs in broadcasting, talking to the people who make the laws and regulations for mobile networks, radio and television.

It was surreal. These were the people I had railed against for much of my broadcasting career. They didn't look scary at all; in fact, they seemed quite lovely. The chairperson welcomed us, and we began our presentation with some video clips I had recorded in Tembisa the Saturday before – fortuitously, at a gathering of township entrepreneurs who were all struggling to grow their businesses because of high data costs. Without following the proper form and protocol, I immediately provided some context for the videos. The MPs laughed. Apparently you have to address the chair formally before you can begin, but we weren't there as politicians, and so they forgave us.

Touch took the committee through the genesis of the #DataMustFall campaign, of which we had unwittingly become leaders. He explained that the campaign was not hostile and that we wouldn't be marching on any network head offices or destroying any property. This was roundly welcomed by the committee because earlier that day Wits University had erupted into violence over the #FeesMustFall protest. We talked about the cost of running a business in the digital realm, about the possibilities that cheaper data might present to young and old, rich and poor. For anyone in the 21st century, a data connection provides immediate access to information, opportunity, employment and the means of connecting with other people. There has never been a more powerful tool for government to prioritise for the empowerment of its citizens.

By the time you read this, data prices may have come down. If we played some small part in making that happen, then I am immeasurably proud that our young business was at the forefront of promoting the people's right to cheaper data. The revolution has truly begun.

Commercial radio is undergoing seismic changes. You can see this in the revisions in the RAMS (Radio Audience Measurement Survey), SABC's 90 per cent local-content quota, the collapse of credibility of SABC management and research that shows that people under the age of 30 are paying less and less attention to traditional media. With the move to digital media, we've contemplated our timing, and many experts have told us that we're too far ahead of the curve to be considered mainstream. It would seem, even conservatively, that this debate can now be put to bed.

By the way, did you manage to look up the seven dirty words that, according to George Carlin, you aren't supposed to say on television (or radio)? Shit, piss, fuck, cunt, cocksucker, motherfucker and tits. But, really, 'tits' doesn't belong there, does it?

Postscript

Why This Is the Best Time to Be Alive

Think about it … you are the luckiest human your family tree has ever produced. No ancestor of yours ever had as much knowledge, opportunity and potential as you have. I know those are bold claims, and there are many things you see every night in the news and on Twitter that might persuade you that things are very bad, but they're really not. What I'm about to tell you isn't fluff or the kind of rubbish motivational speakers churn out to make people feel good, it's the truth, the whole truth and nothing but the truth.

One day, when I'm not too old and hopefully very rich, I'll teach kids history. I love history so much because it was the only subject we had at school that actually taught us about people. It's hard to be a human, whether you're trying to find a job, start a business, raise a family or do something grand, and it's easy to get bogged down in day-to-day stuff and forget the big picture. So let me give you a few facts to make the good days great and the bad days better:

We're living longer. For the past 180 000 years of human existence, the average lifespan used to be about 30 years. People would be married in their teens and anyone who got past 40 would have been a village elder. The average human lifespan in 2016 is over 72 years, and increasing.

We're safer. For most of human history, *at least* 15 per cent of us died violently – one in six of us was murdered or killed in war. Now it's six to eight people per 100 000 worldwide. That's extraordinary. Despite the scary headlines, we're more secure than at any other time since we started walking upright, and definitely better than before that.

In 1986, there were over 70 000 nuclear warheads, armed and ready to turn the whole earth into a big glass crater. Luckily that crisis was largely averted and today there are only about 20 000. Don't get me wrong, that's still too many, but it's progress in the right direction.

We're eating better. Despite every dietician on the planet telling you about paleo, banting, vegan and protein diets, since the 1960s the amount of food available per person has gone up by a quarter. Even though there are more of us, the amount of food we produce is adequate for everyone, even if it's unevenly distributed.

Populations are still growing, but they're slowing down, and more women than ever before are now in a position to choose when and whether they want kids. In 1960, the average woman had 4.5 children; now it's 2.5 (according to Unicef). This has the greatest civilising effect of all upon any society.

The poor are getting less poor. Global inequality is falling – and the developed world is developing faster. In South Africa, more than 8 million people receive social grants and welfare. Before, they had nothing.

We're getting smarter. In universities in Europe, they've had to re-calibrate the IQ tests. One hundred is meant to be the average score. If you score over 100, you're considered smarter than average. If we did IQ tests from the 1950s now, we'd all score an average of 118. It's an established fact that all the knowledge the average man or woman in the 1700s had during the course of their lives would fit on the front page of just one of our daily newspapers today.

We're running things better. Back in 1900 there were only 11 democracies in the whole world. There are over 90 today. That's a lot of people who are empowered to politically influence their destinies.

Look, it's not perfect, but as Winston Churchill said, 'democracy is the worst system of government, except for all the others'.

Technology is exponentially increasing our ability both to do more and to end up doing less – because ultimately the machines will take care of a lot of the work. Drones with HD cameras are mapping the earth in such detail that farmers can use them to survey their entire farm in just a few minutes. They can be programmed to follow you on a run, avoid obstacles, deliver packages and even provide point-to-point human transport. I love that, because it means no more traffic! Imagine swarms of drones doing coordinated tasks such as herding livestock or constructing dwellings. They're already working on it.

Author and futurologist Ray Kurzweil says nanobots half the size of a single red blood cell may soon intelligently destroy disease and repair cells on a molecular level. They'll restore you to perfect health every night while you sleep, and detect and eliminate cancer cells and dangerous DNA mutations on site, in your tissue, without the need for invasive surgery. You'll produce just about no waste because the bots will take the waste and rebuild the ingredients into useful molecules that your cells need. You will eat only for pleasure. Imagine how this will positively impact on pollution.

The public internet is only 25 years old. According to Eric Schmidt of Google, five years from now everyone on earth will be on the internet. One day, a kind of online Ubernet may exist, where like-minded people can have borderless states and make their own laws and rules without stepping on anyone else's toes. Your fridge, front door, heater and TV will all be able to communicate with each other and switch on while you're driving home, so you'll never fumble with keys, shiver in the winter or run out of milk again. Your fridge, by the way, will sense there's not enough milk and order it online. In 2012, to demonstrate these capabilities, an astronaut on the International Space Station controlled a robot in Germany via the internet.

Education will almost certainly take place online, and universities and schools will be wherever you are. You'll be tested and assessed with pinpoint accuracy, enabling you to find the job you want and do it best.

Virtual reality will, in the not-too-distant future, give us the ability to show each other what we actually mean – to copy and paste and transplant experiences and memories. Confusion and ignorance will be reduced to marginal levels – and you can imagine the benefits of that. Husbands will understand wives, and countries will know what other states are going through – so empathy and respect will be built in to every conversation. I know it sounds far-fetched, but think about it. If I can upload your experiences and experience them from your point of view, I'll have just about no reason to hate or ignore you. Microscopic aerial nanobots could swarm and form clouds, or 'foglets', that could create real visual, auditory and tactile environments all around you. You'd never know the difference between them and reality. They're already working on foglets that could simulate solids, liquids and gases, and elastic, hard or soft substances. Imagine your car's seat belt forming automatically around you out of thin air.

One day, you'll be able to upload your entire brain and use an avatar, just like in the movie *Avatar*. This also means that, long after all of us are gone, people in the future will be able to download our experiences and memories and incorporate them into *their* experiences. I know this is sounding a little weird, and you might even be getting uncomfortable, but if we do all of these things right, we eliminate so much of what is negative about the human experience. Keep an open mind …

Heads-up displays, beamed onto the lens of your eye would enable you to have any information whenever you need it, without the need for other devices. Self-driving cars, energy-storing solar panels and 3-D printers will solve almost all our transport, energy and manufacturing needs. They'll even grow meat in laboratories, so no animals need to be killed for food.

And here's the best news of all: wars will become a thing of the past. With so many of our problems solved, governments will shrink and likely only matter at the community level. Gold and diamonds will be manufactured, not mined. In fact, you'll probably be able to atomically construct any element in the periodic table. The whole system that creates wealth and poverty will change, and scarcity won't be the basis for currency.

You won't have to have sex with a real person. For some people, that's not a future they want, but with virtual reality you could probably have sex with anyone you want and they'd never even know. I'll stop now, I might be freaking you out …

The job descriptions of the future haven't been written yet. Nobody can teach you what you will need to learn. Be open to change, be ready to take risks and don't get caught up in negative news stories, racial and political arguments, or religious dogmatism. Those things will pull you back into our horrible, violent, myopic and shitty past. Step into the future with confidence.

Don't forget, you're about to become the best *Homo sapiens sapiens* that your family ever produced, and you're alive at a time when you're more free to express yourself than ever before, more free to be yourself than ever before. You're more free to be … and you can complete that sentence on your own.

Jumping off the cliff is the most terrifying and the most satisfying thing I've ever done. The fall is harrowing, but the challenge focuses you and gives you a reason to get up and do amazing things every day. When you're faced with your own personal cliff, you have more options than just fight or flight, and who knows what you might invent on that exciting journey.

And we're just getting started.

Acknowledgements

This book would never have happened if it weren't for Rina Broomberg. I was (and remain) very reticent to do anything even slightly auto-biographical, especially because I'm not even 40. Perhaps I'm hoping my best stories will come after I turn 40. Rina hounded me until we had a manuscript, and publisher Jeremy Boraine prevailed upon us for some years to get a book out ... and eventually he won. Thanks to my editor, Alfred LeMaitre, and the team at Jonathan Ball Publishers, who quietly made it all happen.

A special mention to my family, who started this tale with me all those years ago ... they are always at the forefront of my life while keeping behind the scenes.

Most of all, thanks to each and every one of you who have shared this journey with me, those who wake up with me every morning on the radio, who follow me on social media and who have weathered the *Idols* seasons with me for so many years. The best is yet to come!